TODAY'S CIVIL SERVICE

A guide to its work with Parliament and Industry

Edited by Dermot Englefield
Deputy Librarian, House of Commons

For the Industry and Parliament Trust

Longman

Today's Civil Service: A Guide to its work with Parliament and Industry

Published by Longman Group Ltd
Longman House
Burnt Mill
Harlow
Essex CM20 2JE
United Kingdom

British Library Cataloguing in Publication data

Today's Civil Service: a guide to its work
with Parliament and industry.
1. Civil Service——Great Britain
I. Englefield, Dermot J.T. II. Industry
and Parliament Trust
354.41006 JN425

ISBN 0-582-90336-X

Typeset by The Word Factory Ltd, Rossendale, Lancashire
Printed in Great Britain by Robert Hartnoll (1985) Ltd, Bodmin

CONTENTS

APPENDICES

Government information for industry

PREFACE

During the winter of 1983/84 the Industry and Parliament Trust ran two well attended seminars on the subject *Understanding the Civil Service*. When I examined the transcripts with a view to editing them, it became clear that certain additions were needed in order to round out the original talks – if they were to be considered for publication. This additional material consists of chapter 4 on civil service training, chapter 7 on the civil service's role of informing Parliament, chapter 10 on the private sector's view of the Civil Service and finally chapter 12 a case study of government support for industry. In addition I planned five appendices, four of which have been prepared by the Department of Trade and Industry and the final one by a colleague in the House of Commons, appendices which are designed for everyday use.

This is a practical book, the work, except for the chapter by Dr. Grant, of practitioners or those with extensive recent experience in the worlds of the Civil Service, of Parliament or of industry. Like a previous Industry and Parliament Trust publication on the new House of Commons Departmental Select Committees, its object is to help these different worlds to understand and work with each other, whether at the level of appreciating their different cultures (chapters 2, 9 and 10) or simply of securing the right telephone number or the required publication (the Appendices).

A society such as ours, where specialist group traditions are now so deeply embedded, differs from that of a century ago when the nation was run by a smaller and far more homogeneous group. Today therefore it is more likely that disparate sections such as those discussed in this book will find it more difficult and yet more necessary to work together. If this book leads to a better understanding and improved working relationship between them, then the object of the original seminars will have been more widely disseminated to the satisfaction of the authors, the Industry and Parliament Trust and the editor. Even more important, I hope that its publication may be helpful to the new readership.

I would like to thank the individual contributors who accepted my editing with hardly a quiver. This especially includes the staff of the Department of Trade and Industry who worked on the important but necessarily humdrum text of Appendices 1–4. To those I would add three colleagues in the House of Commons Library Robert Twigger, Sylvia Warren and Marion Chantry whom the Industry and Parliament Trust commissioned to prepare appendix 5 and the main text respectively. Finally my thanks goes to Susan

Richards of Longman and Fredrick Hyde-Chambers the Secretary of the Industry and Parliament Trust both of whom were that mixture of ready yet unobtrusive support which any editor is happy to find.

Dermot Englefield
Crystal Palace
New Year's Day, 1985

INDUSTRY AND PARLIAMENT TRUST

25 Victoria Street, London SW1H OEX
President: The Rt. Hon. Bernard Weatherill, MP
Speaker of the House of Commons

The Trust, which is a non-profit making registered educational charity, was established in 1977 to make a positive contribution towards improving mutual understanding between industry and members of both Houses of Parliament and the European Parliament. It is strictly non-partisan, is not a lobbying organization and is completely independent of any other organization. At the time this book went to press the Trustees were: The Rt. Hon. The Lord Irving of Dartford DL (Chairman); The Rt. Hon. Lord Carr of Hadley; John Cartwright MP; Jim Craigen MP; The Lord Scanlon; The Rt. Hon. Baroness Seear PC; The Rt. Hon. Viscount Tonypandy PC; Bowen Wells MP.

Objects (i) To enable members of both Houses of Parliament and of the European Parliament to widen their experience in, and increase their knowledge of, industry. (ii) To improve the understanding of industrial managers concerning the problems of Parliament in dealing with matters affecting industry.

Fellowship scheme Fellowships are offered to MPs of all parties who then undertake an integrated 25-day study course with one of the Trust's member companies, seeing for themselves how industry works, how it is affected by legislation, what relationships are really like and how decisions are reached at all levels. Fellow are placed with companies, either singly or in pairs, and their courses are spread over about a year.

Fellows out-of-pocket expenses are met from Trust funds. There is no financial arrangement between the companies and the fellows attached to it.

Seminars for industrialists These seminars are arranged specifically for senior industrialists. They have covered such topics as *Understanding Parliament*, *Understanding the European Community*, *Understanding the new Parliamentary Select Committees* and *Understanding the Civil Service*. The speakers have all been authorities in their particular fields, talking not about political policies, but about their own work and how it relates to the function of Parliament and the problems of industry.

Seminars for parliamentarians As some members find it difficult to undertake a 25-day commitment for a fellowship programme, the Trust holds occasional seminars at the House of Commons open to all parliamentarians. These provide an opportunity to bring together experts from industry, the academic world and Parliament to discuss such subjects as "British Multinationals Overseas", "The Social and Industrial Implications of the Microchip", "The Educational Needs of Industry", and "Industrial Relations and the Economy".

Corporate membership Currently there are 33 companies in full membership with the Trust (from the private and public sectors) and five small business member companies (200 employees or less). They finance the Trust by means of an annual subscription.

Overseas The Trust is apparently the first organization of its kind in the world and after studying its activities, Finland, Sweden, Norway, Belgium and the Netherlands have established parallel bodies, and other countries have pilot schemes under way.

NOTES ON CONTRIBUTORS

Dermot Englefield joined the House of Commons Library in 1954 and has been Deputy Librarian since 1976. He has acted as consultant to the Council of Europe (1970), the European Parliament (1973), the abortive Scottish Assembly (1978) and the Northern Ireland Assembly (1982). He is editor of the microfilm edition of the Printed Records of the Parliament of Ireland 1613–1800 and author of Parliament and Information: the Westminster Scene (1981). Recently he has edited *Commons Select Committees: Catalysts for Progress?* Longman (1984) and with Gavin Drewry, *Information Sources in Politics and Political Science: A survey worldwide,* Butterworths (1984). A study of the relationship of Government and Parliament *Whitehall and Westminster* is to be published shortly, Longman (1985).

John Bourn is visiting Professor in Public Administration, London School of Economics and a Deputy Secretary in the Northern Ireland Office. Prior to that he held the following posts: Assistant Under-Secretary of State, Ministry of Defence 1977–83; Under-Secretary, Northern Ireland Office, 1974–77; Assistant Secretary, Ministry of Defence, 1972–74; Assistant Secretary and Director of Programmes, Civil Service College 1969–72; Private Secretary to Permanant Under-Secretary, Ministry of Defence, 1964–69.

William J.L. Plowden is Director-General of the Royal Institute of Public Administration. He is visiting Professor in Government, London School of Economics; and previously was Under-Secretary, Department of Industry, 1977–78; Central Policy Review Staff, Cabinet Office, 1971–77; Lecturer in Government, 1965–71; and in the Board of Trade 1960–65.

Peter Le Cheminant CB is Director General of the General Council of British Shipping. He was Second Permanent Secretary, Management and Personnel Office, 1983–84 and previously held the following posts: Deputy Secretary, HM Treasury, (Civil Service Department), 1981–83; Deputy Secretary, Cabinet Office, 1978–81; Deputy Secretary, Department of Energy, 1974-77; Under-Secretary, Department of Trade and Industry, 1971–74: He held various appointments with the Ministry of Power, later of Technology, 1968–71: He was Private Secretary to the Prime Minister 1965–68.

Dennis Trevelyan CB has been First Civil Service Commissioner and Deputy Secretary, Management and Personnel Office, since 1983. He entered Home Office, 1950 and has held the following posts: Treasury, 1953–54: Secretary to Parliamentary Under-Secretary of State, Home Office, 1954–55; Principal Private Secretary to Lord President of Council and Leader of House, 1964–67; Assistant Secretary, 1966; Under-Secretary, Northern Ireland Office, 1972–76; Home Office; Under-Secretary, Broadcasting Department, 1976–77; Deputy Secretary and Director-General, Prison Service, 1978–83.

Rt. Hon. Charles Morris is Political Consultant to the Communication Workers Union. He left the House of Commons at the 1983 election. Previously he had been Minister of State, Civil Service Department, 1974–79: Deputy Shadow Leader of the House, 1980–83; Minister of State, Department of the Environment, 1974; PPS to Rt. Hon. Harold Wilson, MP, 1970–74; Deputy Chief Whip, 1969–70; Vice-Chamberlain, HM Household 1967–69; PPS to Postmaster General, 1964. He was a Member, Post Office Workers' Union National Executive Council, 1959–63. Labour Member for Openshaw, Manchester, 1963–83 and a Fellow of the Industry and Parliament Trust.

Rt. Hon. Sir Edward du Cann MP was Chairman, Treasury and Civil Service Affairs Select Committee, 1979–83 and Chairman, Liaison Committee of Select Committee Chairmen, 1980–83. He has also been visiting Fellow, University of Lancaster Business School, 1970–82. Chairman, Public Accounts Committee, 1974–79; first Chairman, Select Committee on Public Expenditure, 1971–72; Chairman, 1972–84 of the "1922" Committee of Conservative backbenchers; Trade Minister, 1963–4; Economic Secretary, Treasury, 1962–63. Conservative Member for Taunton since 1956. Deputy Chairman, Lonrho; Chairman, Cannon Assurance, 1972–80; Keyser Ullman Holdings, 1970–75 and other companies.

Dr. Wyn Grant is Senior Lecturer in Politics, University of Warwick. He is also Associate Editor, *Political Studies*; co-author, *The CBI*, 1977; author, *Independent Local Politics in England and Wales*, 1977; *The Political Economy of Industrial Policy*, 1982 and is currently co-writing *The Politics of Economic Policy*. He has written numerous contributions to publications on government-industry relations, including a recent study of government relations departments in large British firms. He is the British participant in a ten country International Institute of Management project on the associative action of business in western societies.

Glyn England was Chairman, Central Electricity Generating Board, 1977–82. He is Consultant to the World Bank with particular reference to relationships between public institutions and ministers. He is Director, F.H. Lloyd (Holdings). Previously he was Chairman, South Western Electricity Board, 1973–77; Director-General South Western Region, 1971–73; Chief Operations Engineer, CEGB 1966–71; Vice-President, International Union of Producers and Distributors of Electrical Energy 1981–; Member of the British National Committee, World Energy Conference, 1977. He was sometime Labour Member Herts CC.

Sir Kenneth Corfield is Chairman and Managing Director of Standard Telephones and Cables plc. He has been Vice-President, ITT Europe Inc., since 1967; Chairman of the British Engineering Council, since 1981; Managing Director, K.G. Corfield Limited, 1950–60; Executive Director, Parkinson Cowan, 1960–66; Deputy Chairman, Standard Telephones and Cables Limited, 1969–79. Director: Midland Bank Limited, 1979–; Britoil plc, 1982–. Chairman, EDC for Ferrous Foundries Industry, 1975–78. Member: Advisory Council, Science Museum, 1975–; Vice-President, Engineering Employers' Federation, 1979–; Member Council: CBI, 1971–; Institute of Directors, 1981–; Vice-President, BIM, 1978–. Hon. Fellow, Sheffield Polytechnic. Hon. DSc: City University 1981; Bath University, 1982; Hon. DScEng London University 1982. His publications include *Product Design*, Report for NEDO, 1979; *No Man An Island*, 1982.

Anne E. Mueller CB is Second Permanent Secretary, Cabinet Office (Management and Personnel Office). Prior to that she was Deputy Secretary, Department of Trade and Industry, 1970–84, and has been Director, European Investment Bank, 1978–84 with the Department of Industry 1970–84. Previously held posts in Ministry of Technology, Department of Economic Affairs, HM Treasury, OEEC and the Ministry of Labour.

Nigel East writes on applications of new technology for the Information Division of the Department of Trade and Industry. The work involves close collaboration with companies like Shelley Thermoformers.

Roger Hird is a Principal in the Department of Trade and Industry currently responsible for sponsoring the machine tool industry.

Robert Twigger is a Senior Library Clerk in the Statistical Section of the Research Division of the House of Commons Library

FOREWORD

The two great foundations for the future well being of the people in this country are, on the one hand, Government and Civil Service, and on the other industry and commerce. The mutual understanding between these two groups is crucial if the nation is to produce the wherewithal upon which all else depends. Our only limitation to doing good is the ability to provide the wherewithal with which to do it.

All our experience in The Industrial Society is that the current generation of civil servants has seen why industry matters and has realised the urgency of developing a more productive relationship between industry, Civil Service and Government.

For several years, the Industry and Parliament Trust has helped MP's to understand the role of industry by attachments to companies. What good news it is that as a result, of these attachments, a group of the Trust's member companies now aranges similar selected secondments for senior civil servants. The more each of us understands the role of the other, the more productive is our relationship likely to be. Let us hope such attachments can be extended, so civil servants at many different levels and from different parts of the country can have the opportunity to discover more about industry and commerce.

Many managers and union leaders remain sceptical of the role of Government and of the Civil Service. It has never been so important for Whitehall to understand fully the world of industry and commerce, and to bridge the gap between industry and the government of the day. However, it is up to all of us to take practical steps to build a better relationship – for on this, the future of industry and commerce depends.

I therefore welcome this book, as a timely reminder for all of us of how the Civil Service can act as the catalyst between industry and Parliament. I hope many readers will use *Today's Civil Service* as a spur to taking further practical action themselves, to build an even closer relationship and to face the challenges of the future.

John Garnett, CBE
Director
The Industrial Society

1

THE CIVIL SERVICE

Chapter 1

Structure and Responsibilities
John Bourn

Chapter 2

The Culture of Whitehall
William Plowden

Chapter 3

Recent Developments
Peter Le Cheminant CB

Chapter 4

Training for the Future
Dennis Trevelyan CB

1

STRUCTURE AND RESPONSIBILITIES

JOHN BOURN

I want to start by describing the size and structure of the Civil Service.

Figure 1 shows the size of the Civil Service within the public sector as a whole. It is important to distinguish civil servants from local authority employees, and also from national health service employees. The public sector can be defined in a number of ways. Under the definition in Figure 1 it comes to about 4½ million out of a total United Kingdom working population of some 24 million. If we include nationalised industries and the armed forces, however, it comes to about 7 million out of 24 million.

FIGURE 1 Public Sector Employment 1970–84

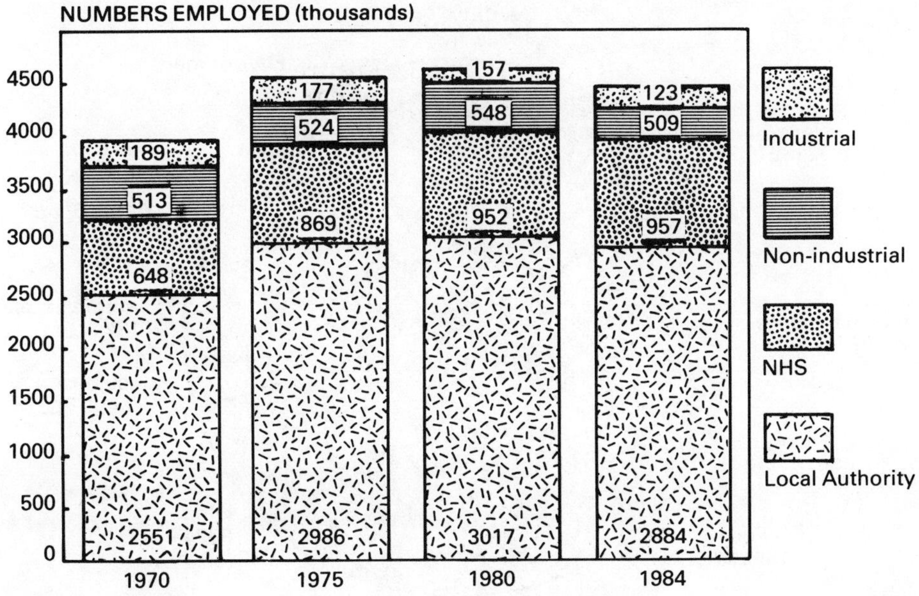

Within the Civil Service there is a distinction between industrial and non-industrial staff. The industrial Civil Service consists of people who work in the Royal Dockyards, in the Royal Parks and in similar jobs. The non-industrial Civil Service consists of the people traditionally seen as civil servants – such as the office staff of the Inland Revenue, the Treasury, the Ministry of Agriculture, Fisheries and Food and other departments; in short, the policy advisers to Ministers, as well as the great majority of civil servants who are carrying out government decisions.

The total size of the Civil Service, industrial and non-industrial, as set out in Figure 1, came to 633,000 on 1 January 1984, to 624,000 on 1 April 1984, and 617,000 on 1 October 1984. In May 1979 there were 732,000; this represents a 15% reduction and means that the Government more than achieved the target of a 100,000 cut in the Civil Service in its first five years in office.

The reduction in the top three grades has been 16% while the reduction in clerical staff has been about 9%. The so-called mandarins in Whitehall have therefore been more affected than most. The Government has recently set a new target to reach 593,000 by 1 April 1988. This will represent a 21% reduction in the Civil Service over twelve years.

How have the cuts been made? Lord Gowrie, the Chancellor of the Duchy of Lancaster, explained in the House of Lords on 5 December 1984 that well over half the cuts had been achieved by

FIGURE 2 Non-Industrial Staff by Department 1984

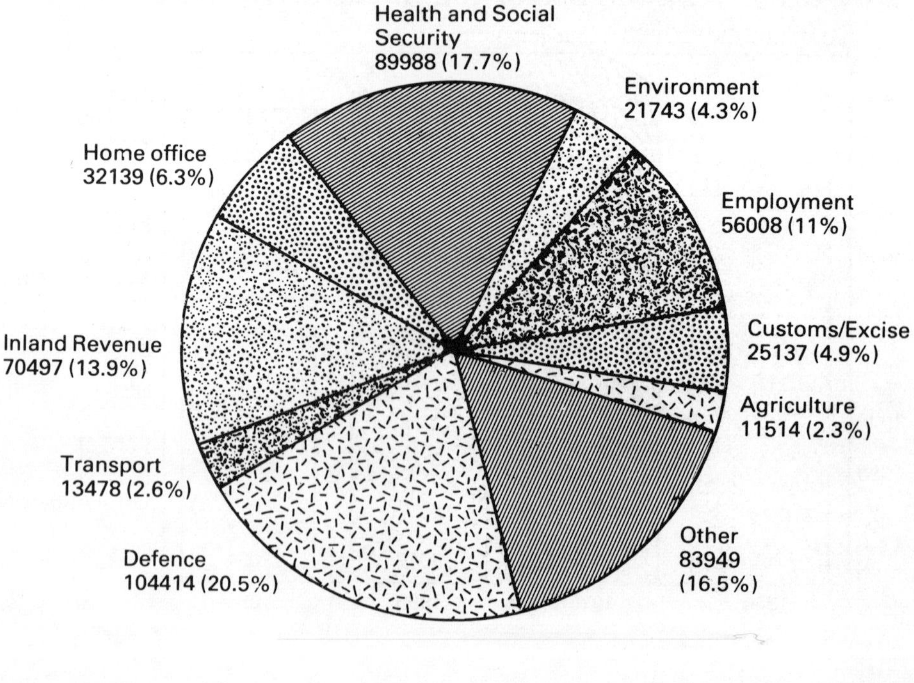

greater efficiency; some 20% had been achieved by dropping or materially curtailing functions; some 10% by privatisation including contracting out; and about 2% by hiving off to new and existing public sector bodies.

Figure 2 illustrates how the non-industrial Civil Service is split between departments. The most striking feature is the size of defence; some 20% of non-industrial civil servants and 32% of all civil servants work in the Ministry of Defence. This is not because of any increase in numbers stemming from the present Government's increase in the size of our defence effort; indeed, the cut in the numbers of defence staff between 1979 and 1984 has been about 20%, which is greater than the cut overall. But defence is a major function, which employs many people in the administration of the armed forces, together with weapons procurement.

The second biggest group of staff is concerned with paying pensions and benefits of various kinds, some 90,000 being employed on this task. There are also some very small departments. The smallest that I have been able to find is the Law Officers' Department which works for the Attorney General and Solicitor General and consists of just 20 people. So there is a very wide spread in the numbers in different Departments.

FIGURE 3 Non-Industrial Staff by Region 1984

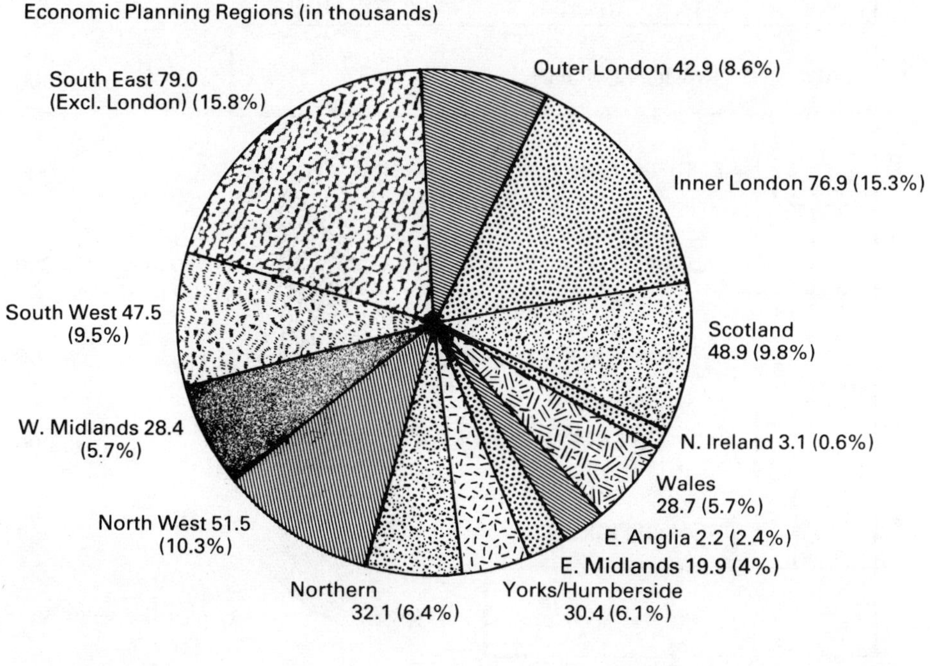

Where do all these people work? Figure 3 shows the distribution of non-industrial civil servants round the country. As you would expect with non-industrial civil servants, there is a fairly large concentration – about 15% – in the inner London area; defined as within five miles of Charing Cross. But it is by no means the case that all civil servants work in Whitehall. The chart shows their wide distribution throughout Great Britain. This reflects two facts. First, many functions need to be conducted throughout the country as a whole, such as the employment and the social security work. Secondly, the distribution represents the results of a deliberate policy in years past to disperse civil servants and their work away from London and to locate them in other parts of the country, especially in those areas which would benefit most from extra employment and consequential expenditure in the regions. To some extent this dispersal policy has been overtaken by the reduction in the size of the Civil Service in recent years.

FIGURE 4 Non-Industrial Staff Structure 1984

Main groups, classes and grades

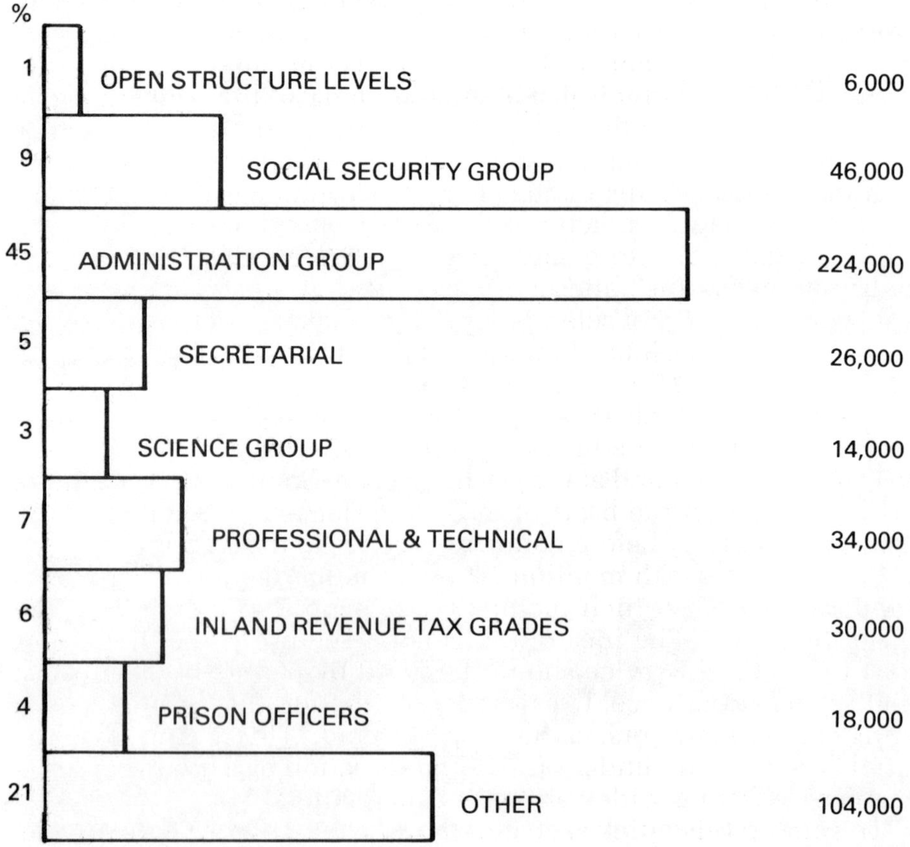

Figure 4 is concerned with structure. The Civil Service is organised in a series of categories and groups, broadly speaking in terms of the original education and subsequent training and of the basic functions of the civil servants concerned. There are too many to show them all on one chart, but I have picked out some of the larger ones. By far the largest is the Administration Group, some 224,000, which includes the generality of civil servants engaged in policy advice and implementation. Most of the civil servants in this Group – some 65% – are people at the lower clerical levels concerned with the processing of applications for licences, the handling of work in employment offices and so on – the normal work of clerks. Then there is the science group of 14,000. The majority are in the defence field, but others work in such places as medical research laboratories. Professional and technical staff include a large number in civil engineering activities, technical drawing and design, and the oversight of the construction of buildings of various sorts. Among the other groups of staff I would pick out inspectorates as a particularly important group. Perhaps we think mainly of income tax inspectors with whom we all deal. But there are also inspectors of schools and inspectors of factories, both representing an important and interesting element of British government. The concept of the inspector is verymuch a nineteenth century one, though it is just as relevant today – the man or woman appointed to ensure that standards and rules laid down in Acts of Parliament are maintained, and to promote good administration. In addition, other groups of staff include psychologists, economists, statisticians, lawyers, actuaries, and customs and excise officers. The essential point to grasp is that the Civil Service consists not only of "mandarins" and counter clerks but also contains a very substantial number of scientists, professional and technical people, inspectors of various kinds, and many others with special knowledge and skills.

The way in which these groups are organised allows for their recruitment at three educational levels corresponding essentially to O level, A level, and at the graduate level. Some civil servants are also recruited on the basis of their experience and attainments in other walks of life before coming into the Civil Service.

Finally, it is worth mentioning in particular the top six grades of the Civil Service, which include 6,200 people, and constitute the Open Structure. The idea of the Open Structure is that the senior jobs in the Civil Service should be filled by people of the greatest ability and experience, irrespective of whether they started as scientists, administrators, or in another field. This means that the Civil Service is run under Ministerial direction by a group comprising people from a wide variety of backgrounds.

To sum up this quick sketch of the structure of the Civil Service;

people will join a particular category or group and their careers are, for the most part, likely to be within the group that they join. But the variety of jobs is considerable; there is movement between the categories and groups; and the Open Structure at the top is open on merit to people from all backgrounds.

FIGURE 5 Non-Industrial Staff by Age 1984

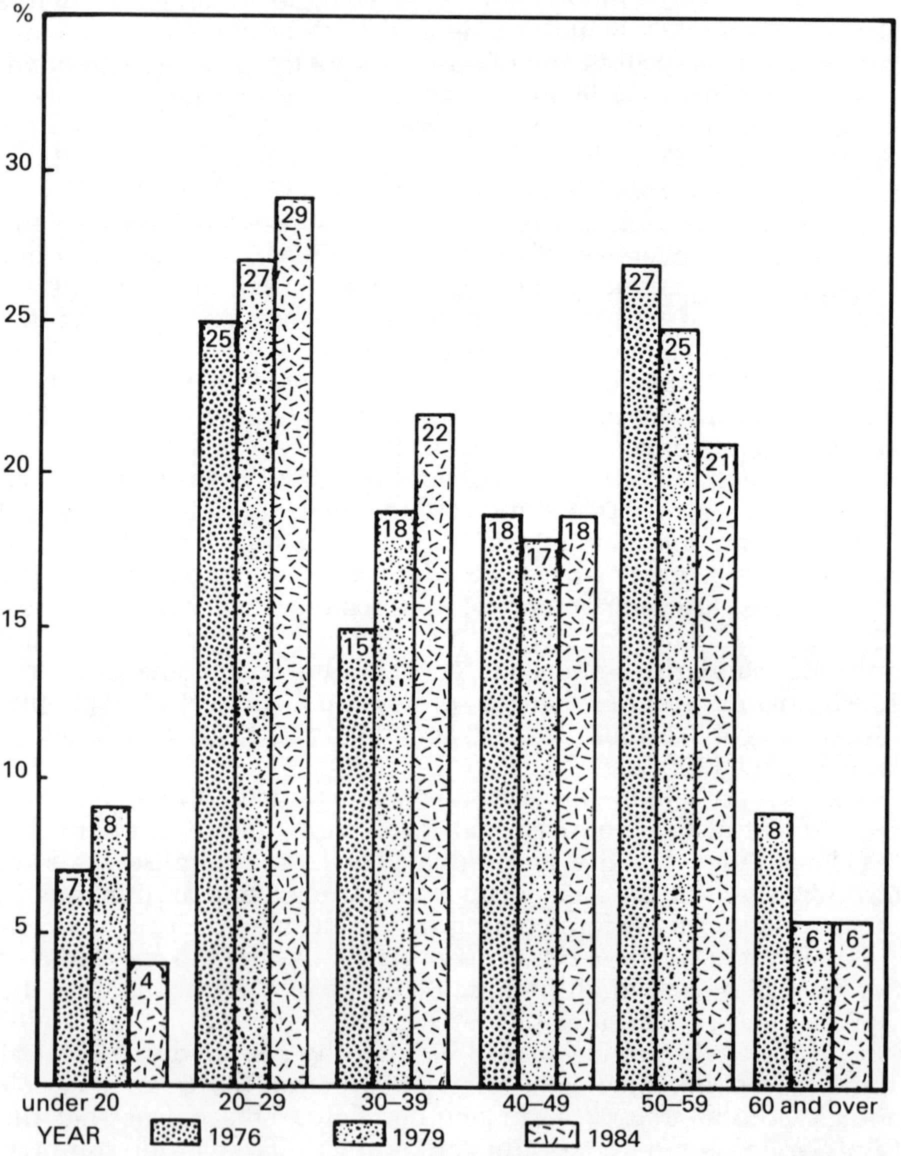

Figure 5 shows the age structure of the Civil Service. Two age groups, the under-30s and the fifties to sixty, are very strongly represented. The older group represents the considerable recruitment which took place in the years after the second world war with the coming of the welfare state and general extension of the role of government. The younger group represents the increase in Civil Service numbers – it is also true of local government employees – in the period up to the mid seventies. A large number of retirements will take place over the next few years, which may go some way to soften the blow to the people who feel that their career prospects may be diminished by the reduction in the size of the Civil Service.

FIGURE 6 Non-Industrial Staff by Sex

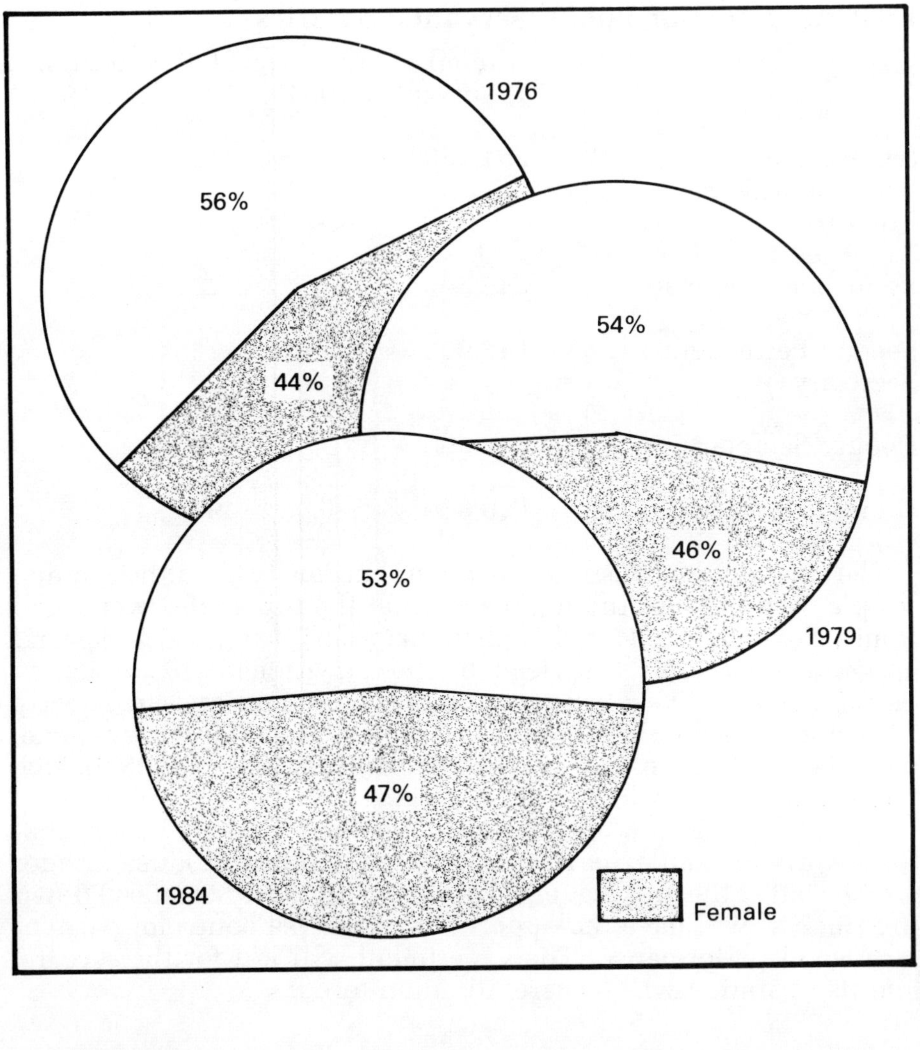

The breakdown of the Civil Service by sex set out in Figure 6 is interesting. In 1976, 44% of civil servants were women; by 1984 they numbered 47%. As in other organisations, the women are disproportionately represented at the lower levels, in the secretarial group, and as the clerical officers and clerical assistants; they are not so well represented at senior levels. This is a common pattern in many occupations in western societies, though it would be outside this Chapter's remit to debate the reasons for it. Certainly, the Civil Service has as its principle the opening of careers to all talents, irrespective of sex or race. Although a number of other employers have caught up over the years, the Civil Service was originally in the vanguard in opening job opportunities to women.

FIGURE 7 Senior Public Servants' Salaries

	Annual Salary 1 November 1984	Staff in post at 1 October 1984
Secretary of the Cabinet Permanent Secretary to the Treasury	£51,250	2
Permanent Secretary	£45,500	23
Second Permanent Secretary	£42,000	13
Deputy Secretary	£36,500	140
Under Secretary	£29,500[1]	496

The final Figure caters for the natural curiosity about how much people earn. It gives the figures of what the top grades were paid from 1 November 1984, although higher salaries are paid for special appointments. Thus the Head of the Government Accountancy Service, on a four year contract, is paid £75,000 per annum – nearly 50% more than the Head of the Civil Service – and Mr Peter Levene, who became Chief of Defence Procurement in March 1985 for five years will be paid £95,000 per annum.

An interesting new development on Civil Service pay is that from April 1985 an experimental scheme will be introduced under which staff at the grading levels of Grade 3 (Under Secretary) down to Principal will have the opportunity to earn a bonus for particularly good performance. The experiment will last for three years, and its operation will be carefully monitored.

Internal Organisation of Departments

We turn now to the internal organisation of departments. Given the extraordinary variety of work in the Civil Service, there is no common form of departmental structure. The organisation of a tax office will be quite different from that of a research team looking into missile technology. Three points about the organisation of departments are important. First, Civil Service organisation is fairly formal. There are clear lines of command and control. This is not only a good management precept but it is also particularly significant in the context of parliamentary government. Ministers – and civil servants are there to support their Ministers – are personally and collectively responsible to Parliament. It is important, for example, that in financial matters it should always be possible to say who authorised expenditure, on what authority, and for what purpose. It is also important that Ministers should be able to respond to Parliament at question time and during debates. This is easier to arrange if there are clear lines of command and control.

The second point qualifies the first. Formal organisation does not mean that everybody occupies a place in a rigid hierarchy and that the papers rise up and down these hierarchies, only being exchanged between them at the highest levels. The work of civil servants requires cooperation, the contribution of people with a variety of expertise-financial, legal, engineering for example – who work together in project teams and groups so as to try to secure that the work is done as effectively as possible.

The third point concerns the changes that have been introduced in the working of the Civil Service and the structure of departments during the present Conservative Administration, from 1979 onwards. There has been particular emphasis on ensuring, throughout the Civil Service, that the objectives and purposes of each division and section are clearly specified, and that each individual has a clearly specified job and a clearly specified level and degree of responsibility. And responsibility generally is being pushed down the hierarchy to where the costs are actually incurred. Finally, departments should operate in the continuing recognition that there is always scope for improvement and greater value for money; that the use of modern methods should be rigorously pursued; that training and information should be provided so that each job may be properly carried out; and that performance should be evaluated against specified standards.

I can give one illustration of how this works in my own area of responsibility, the Northern Ireland Office in Belfast, where my remit is particularly concerned with security. The work is organised and the staff structured in a series of cost centres, covering such areas as prison administration, forensic medicine, and the reform of the criminal law. There are specified objectives for each centre. Each of these cost centres has its own budget, and monitors its out-turn in relation to its particular activities, using performance indicators. During the year, we evaluate the progress of the work to see to what extent the objectives are being achieved, the reasons for any deviations from planned performance, and what remedial action needs to be taken.

This example is worth giving because it shows the application of this new approach to one of the oldest and most traditional functions of government – law and order.

Special and Political Advisers

We now consider some other developments. Ministers of several administrations and different political colours have appointed Special Advisers from outside the Civil Service to provide them with advice on policy questions; we can give examples from the administrations of Mr Macmillan, Mr Lloyd George, and earlier. The purpose of such advisers is either to add a political dimension to the advice normally available to Ministers from career civil servants or to provide expert advice in a particular professional field.

These advisers have direct access to their Ministers and are normally outside the departmental hierarchy. Their status is that of civil servants who are limited-period appointees. As such, they are paid from public funds. But, unlike other appointees who are engaged for a fixed period of time, Special Advisers are appointed for the duration of a particular administration. Their appointment may of course terminate sooner if the particular Minister whom they are serving relinquishes his portfolio.

Guidance on the appointment and conditions of service of Special Advisers is a matter for the Prime Minister. As civil servants in touch with ministers they are expected to conform as closely as possible to the Civil Service rules of conduct including those on political activity. Thus they are debarred from parliamentary candidature under the Servants of the Crown (Parliamentary Candidature) Order 1960 and would be expected to resign before taking part, for example, in a parliamentary by-election campaign. However, ministers have taken the view that, provided possible conflicts of loyalty are avoided, it is not improper for Special Advisers to engage in political life to some degree. Because of the nature of advice they are called upon to provide, they are required to maintain their links with the so-called "grass roots" of their own party and with the party machinery.

A parliamentary question, answered on 10 April 1984, set out in the Notes to this chapter[2], illustrates the position of Special Advisers and the difference between them and Political Advisers.

Are Specialist Advisers a valuable feature of modern government? My answer is "yes"; they come into the Service with a different viewpoint, make a valuable contribution, and can work with civil servants within a department productively, to carry forward the policy of the government of the day.

Central Departments

In this country we have a system of Cabinet government, in which Ministers collectively – and with only rare exceptions – take responsibility in Parliament and in the country for the policy of the government as a whole. The Cabinet itself constitutes a group of Ministers who are seen as responsible for determining government policy, presenting it to Parliament and to the world at large, and who are judged upon it, not only at election time, but through the public and media comments made upon their activities every day.

The major department concerned with servicing the Cabinet is the Cabinet Office; it attends first to the business of producing the minutes of Cabinet meetings, which is important because people should know exactly what has been said and decided. But it is also frequently asked to conduct studies, particularly inter-departmental studies, often through groups of civil servants servicing and supporting ministerial committees. For instance, when we were preparing for United Kingdom entry into the European Communities, the inter-departmental arrangements were spearheaded by the Cabinet Ofice. This is the kind of function that it can perform very well, enabling the government to work collectively rather than as a series of separate departments. The Cabinet Office is mainly staffed by civil servants seconded from other departments.

Several other organisations exist within the Cabinet Office. They include the Central Statistical Office, responsible for the coordination of statistics collected by departments, and for producing and publishing statistics needed for central economic and social policies; and the Management and Personnel Office, responsible for central personnel management policy within the Civil Service including recruiting, training and staff development; and for the promotion of efficiency on subjects of common concern to a range of departments such as contract and procurement procedures.

The other central department is the Treasury, essentially the same as the Ministries of Finance found in other countries the world over. The purpose of the Treasury is to assist the government to control public expenditure and to promote the satisfactory funding of the UK economy. Five main areas or sectors of work may be distinguished. The Public Services Sector is responsible for controlling aggregate public expenditure and for most of the individual public expenditure programmes including manpower and pay. The

Overseas Finance Sector is concerned with balance of payments policies, the management of the reserves, international monetary co-operation, the aid programme and matters connected with UK membership of the European Economic Community.

The Chief Economic Adviser's Sector is responsible for the preparation of short-term and medium-term economic forecasts and for specialist advice on macro-economic policies. The Domestic Economy staffs are concerned with fiscal, monetary and counter-inflation policies, and also with the Treasury's contribution to industrial policies, including control of public expenditure on industry and agriculture. The Pay Sector is responsible for the development of the Civil Service pay system, administers home and overseas allowances, deals with the pay of the armed forces and works closely with the Top Salaries Review Body on such matters as the pay of chairmen and members of public bodies, Government Ministers and MPs.

We read in the papers every year of a great crisis between the Treasury and the so-called "spending departments" as the determination of the annual public expenditure plans takes place. This is often over dramatised. It makes a very good story to conceive a highly emotional argument between one group of people who are concerned to keep spending down and other groups who are determined to push it up. But although this story is presented every year as though it were something special and extraordinary, the process to which it refers is exactly what is to be expected.

As we find in every country, there is a clear connection between the responsibility of ministers to carry forward their programmes and the ability of the country to afford their proposals. It is the job of the Treasury to draw together these requirements and to promote the inter-departmental discussions leading to the annual public expenditure White Paper published at the time of the Budget, which shows the Government's spending plans in the financial year immediately ahead and the following two years.

Finally, when dealing with coordination within and between Departments, it is important to mention the "Private Office network". Ministers' private secretaries – personal assistants would be the more usual term in the business world – have the job of ensuring that the minister's instructions are properly relayed in his or her Department; that full and timely advice comes forward from the appropriate sections of the Department; that the Minister's Parliamentary and representational duties are properly supported and that information passes as necessary between Ministers in the formulation and execution of government policy. Clearly, ministers' private secretaries have a key role in the system of government – it is a job that requires intelligence, tact and stamina of a high order. But it is not a party political job – the private secretary does not, for example, help the minister with his or her constituency work, or with political speeches at party conferences.

The Civil Service and Parliament

The last subject that I should like to deal with is the Civil Service and Parliament. It is sometimes suggested in newspaper articles and media comment that Parliament, if it ever was significant, no longer has an important place in our scheme of government, having become entirely subordinated to Ministers and civil servants. Even a short experience in Whitehall will make clear how wrong this view is, and how fundamentally important Parliament is in the British constitution. Parliament has a crucial significance in the work of government, and this is shown by the great seriousness with which ministers approach Parliamentary business, their concern that the policies they present to it should be well conceived, and their anxiety that they should give a good account of themselves when they appear before Parliament for questions or for debates.

It is also suggested that civil servants may find some of Parliament's activities "tiresome" in the sense, for example, that all kinds of awkward questions have to be answered at the expense of "getting on with the real work". I completely disagree with this view, because it is essential in a democracy that the legislative assembly should have full rights to ask questions, to debate and to evaluate the performance of ministers and their Departments. I recognise that civil servants may well have to spend a good deal of time proposing answers for their ministers to give to Parliamentary Questions; providing material for debates; and, increasingly frequently today, appearing before Select Committees of Parliament.

Sometimes civil servants may take a drubbing from these Committees. This may not be a very pleasant experience for the individuals concerned, though it will certainly be an incentive for improved performance in the future. Nevertheless, I believe that Parliamentary Questions and debates and the work of Select Committees constitute a most important contribution to the working of our democracy and that, though they may be time consuming and costly, the benefits that are derived from these institutions overwhelmingly justify the time and expense of providing them.

Conclusion

Finally, I would underline the point that, in describing the structure, organisation and operation of the Civil Service, we must never lose sight of the fact that the "machinery of Government" ultimately consists of people who are there to provide a service to the community. They will be able to do this only if we have an understanding of the community at large. The idea of the Civil Service as some kind of cloistered sector of society, with few direct dealings with the wider community, is a bad one as well as an impractical one. Developments in recent years, notably the interchange of staff with the private sector and with other parts of national life, have made a useful contribution to overcoming barriers and misunderstandings. We must make further progress still in this direction.

Notes:
1. This figure attracts London Allowance if appropriate.
2. Parliamentary Questions on Special and Political Advisers

Special and Political Advisers

Mr. Gordon Brown asked the Prime Minister if she will list all the Special Advisers and Political Advisers who have held appointments since May 1979, together with the detailed terms and conditions of employment; and whether in all cases these were in line with paragraphs 9870 and 9874 of the general principles of conduct for civil servants.

The Prime Minister: Since May 1979 the following have served or are serving as Special Advisers or Political Advisers to Ministers:

SPECIAL ADVISERS

Mr. J. Hoskyns	Head of the No. 10 Policy Unit (and subsequently to the Secretary of State for Transport)
Mr. N. Strauss†	Special Adviser to the Prime Minister
Professor A. Walters	Economic Adviser to the Prime Minister
Mr. F. Mount	Head of the No. 10 Policy Unit
Sir Anthony Parsons†	Foreign Affairs Adviser to the Prime Minister
Mr. J. Redwood	No. 10 Policy Unit (currently Head of the Policy Unit)
Sir Percy Cradock†	Foreign Affairs Adviser to the Prime Minister
Mr. P. Shipley	No. 10 Policy Unit
Hon. C. Monckton	No. 10 Policy Unit
Mr. O. Letwin	No. 10 Policy Unit
Mr. D. Hobson*†	No. 10 Policy Unit
Mrs. C. Ryder	Personal Assistant to the Prime Minister
Dame Felicity Yonge	Chief Whip
Mr. D. Howe†	Paymaster General (and subsequently to Lord President of the Council)
Mr. G. Cardona	Financial Secretary, Treasury
Mr. P. Cropper	Chief Secretary, Treasury (and subsequently to Paymaster General*†)

Mr. R. Shepherd	Secretary of State for Employment (and subsequently Secretary of State for Northern Ireland)
Professor R. Dyson†	Secretary of State for Social Services
Mr. I. Heggie†	Secretary of State for Transport
Mr. D. Young*†	Secretary of State for Industry
Mr. D. French	Chief Secretary, Treasury
Mr. S. Sherbourne*	Secretary of State for Industry
Mr. E. Berman†	Secretary of State for the Environment
Dr. L. Rouse	Secretary of State for Energy (and subsequently Financial Secretary, Treasury)
Miss A. Ward	Chief Whip
Mr. R. Lord	Chief Secretary, Treasury
Mr. M. Portillo	Financial Secretary, Treasury
Mr. A. Ridley	Chancellor of the Exchequer
Mrs. K. Ramsay	Secretary of State for Transport
Mr. C.G. Mockler	Secretary of State for the Environment
Sir R. Cooke†	Secretary of State for the Environment
Mr. N. True	Secretary of State for Social Services
Mr. R.D.R. Harris	Home Secretary
Mr. L. Bickham	Secretary of State for Northern Ireland
Mr. J. Houston	Secretary of State for Foreign and Commonwealth Affairs
Mr. S. Sexton	Secretary of State for Education and Science
Mr. M. Dobbs†	Secretary of State for Trade and Industry
Mr. C. Butler†	Secretary of State for Wales
Professor Sir Sam Edwards†	Secretary of State for Energy
Mr. J. Sterling*†	Secretary of State for Trade and Industry
Mr. R. Ehrman†	Secretary of State for Employment
Mr. T. Baron	Secretary of State for the Environment

* Denotes unpaid
† Denotes part-time

Special Advisers are civil servants and their terms of appointment are similar to those of other civil servants and they are subject to the same rules of conduct (including paragraphs 9870 and 9874 of the Civil Service code) apart from the certain exceptions which reflect the special nature of their role.

Political Advisers

No. 10 Downing Street

Mr. D. Wolfson	Chief of Staff
Mr. R. Ryder	Political Secretary
Mr. S. Sherbourne	Political Secretary
Professor Sir Douglas Hague	Political Adviser
Miss C.M. Stevens	Personal Assistant

Department of Employment
Mr. R. Gilbert (part-time)

Political Advisers are not civil servants and are not paid from public funds. Although the provisions of the Civil Service code are not generally appropriate, political advisers are required to avoid conflicts of interest between their work for Ministers and their private and business affairs.

EFFICIENCY ADVISER

In addition, Lord Rayner and Sir Robin Ibbs have held the appointment of Adviser on efficiency.

2

THE CULTURE OF WHITEHALL

William Plowden

This chapter is concerned with the culture of Whitehall. It seems to me to be extremely important to learn, as John Bourn in the previous chapter has told us, how an organisation is structured and what people do, but it is equally important to understand what kind of people they are and how they view the world.

It is clear that one should be extremely wary of generalisations about the Civil Service, in particular generalisations which imply that all civil servants are Whitehall mandarins. None the less, in discussing the culture of Whitehall, I will be dealing largely with mandarins – the upper ranks of the administration group – because it is they who comprise the group that advises ministers, help many to formulate policy and with whom, at senior levels, industrialists and their companies are likely to deal. By world standards, the British Civil Service is extremely good; we are well served. The Civil Service is certainly not responsible for Britain's economic and political decline; it would be foolish to suggest that it is. The results of a survey of the extra- mural activities of Italian civil servants in 1980 make a useful comparison.

1. Those who hardly ever report for work because no checks are made . . . 19%
2. Those selling goods within ministries during working time . . . 33%
3. Those with a second job . . . 54%

I simply underline the point that the British Civil Service is, by world standards, not bad.

The top three grades in Figure 4 (*see* chapter 1) consist of the 800 to 900 most senior civil servants, who are the policy makers. They are a very small proportion of the whole Civil Service, but a considerable influence on policy and the way in which it is made. About two-thirds of them have joined the Civil Service straight from university, characteristically joining younger than civil servants elsewhere in the world; on average two or three years younger for instance than their German counterparts. And they are still disproportionately from Oxford or Cambridge and disproportionately educated in non-technical subjects. They are highly intelligent in a formal academic sense, with good degrees, highly educated then, sensitive and alert. The other third destined for the top posts are promoted from within the Civil Service.

The Civil Service Career

It is important to understand the nature and shape of the civil service career and the way in which it influences the perceptions of civil servants and how they view the world. Here are some points, which though fairly obvious are worth underlining. First, it is still a lifetime career; and there is a high correlation between peoples' seniority and their age. The average age of permanent secretaries and deputy secretaries is about 55 to 56; so the top people are relatively old. The Civil Service puts out admirable statistics about its own manpower, which show that 25 or 30 years work in that single career is not unusual for people who are at the top of the civil service. Secondly, most civil servants – I use the word "most" because if you look at their curricula vitae you will find exceptions – make their careers within a single department. People do move about. The real "high fliers" are often seconded briefly to the Treasury, the Cabinet Office, or Number 10 Downing Street, as the previous chapter mentioned; a slowly growing number, though still too few, are seconded to outside posts in the private sector, in local government and so on. And at the very top – deputy secretary and permanent secretary – a change of department is quite common. But most civil servants spend a lifetime career within a single department – the Home Office, the Department of Trade and Industry and so on. Thirdly, civil servants at the top move relatively rapidly and between unrelated jobs. The average length of tenure of many posts is two years, and in some cases it is as low as a year and a half. Again there are reliable figures to show this. It has not been uncommon in the recent past to find people moving jobs on their way up to the top every two or three years, and even though they may have stayed in the same department, they will often have moved from a job that deals with one topic to a job that deals with something completely different. Moves will be within, for instance, the Home Office or the Department of Trade and Industry, but the content of the jobs will often vary considerably. Fourthly, a familiar point which is underlined by the contrasts that John Bourn has shown concerning the geographical distribution of the Civil Service, the policy makers are largely London-based. Whitehall is in London and people who work in the senior posts make their careers in and around Whitehall. Many civil servants do not move very far, either in where they live or where they work from that magic square mile in the centre of London. Understanding this background to their careers is important in seeing how peoples' perceptions are shaped and the approach they bring to their jobs.

Civil servants have been much criticised during the last 20 years, and indeed for longer. It has been quite common, especially during the 1960s, for this criticism to be from the left of the political spectrum seeing the Civil Service as a privileged bastion holding out against the Socialist revolution. But consider this short quotation from G.D.H. Cole, writing in the early 1940s about the Civil Service of the 1930s.

"I think that the average, highly-placed civil servant has too little experience of being anything except a civil servant, too little knowledge of people outside the narrow group with which he ordinarily mixes in social affairs. I think he is caught too young and trained too thoroughly in the practice of a particular routine. I think he enjoys too much security under conditions which tend to make him erect into an ideal, the negative virtue of never making a mistake. . . ."

It is a theme which one will find repeated again and again. The Fulton Committee of 1968 was one wouldbe turning point in the modernisation of the Civil Service. It repeated many of those criticisms and made many recommendations, some of which have been implemented, many not, in an attempt to try to change the orientation of the Civil Service, to make it more managerial and, less *mandarin* and less *amateur*. Recently there have been the criticisms of Sir John Hoskyns and comments on the inadequacy of management within the Civil Service which have led to significant changes, discussed in chapter 3 and chapter 4. I have mentioned the overwhelming influence of the small group of senior administrators, and, as shown in chapter 1 there are many other groups playing prominent parts in the administration of the country and in the Civil Service, certainly in numerical terms. I would simply offer the prejudiced view that the only really influential group outside the senior administrators are the economists. This is the single specialism which is now accepted in the corridors of policy in Whitehall. Indeed perhaps the single major change in terms of the culture of professionalism in the Civil Service in the last 20 years, has been the way in which the economists have emerged from a back-seat position and now play quite a prominent part in the policy-making process, particularly in the Treasury but also in departments such as Trade and Industry,

Environment, and even Health and Social Security – I say "even" because one would not necessarily think of DHSS as a department for economists. However essentially it is in the small close-knit group of administrators who all know each other and most of whom have been in the civil service for thirty or so years where real influence rests. It is a very difficult system to by-pass with new ideas or propositions.

With regard to skills and working relationships, how do civil servants think of themselves? What is the nature of the task in which they see themselves as excelling or having to excel? It is worth reaffirming that it has been the convention for the higher ranks of the Civil Service to see themselves as advisers not managers. The following passage is taken from a perceptive article written by David Howell, a young civil servant in the Department of Employment group, which was published in the journal *Public Administration*, and compares his own experience as a secondee in Marks & Spencer with his experience as a civil servant.

"For all the emphasis on managerialism in the Fulton Report and after all, most officials see themselves – in many cases correctly – as the confidential advisers of ministers rather than the managers of activities; they look up, not down. Jobs which involve the management of activities therefore command comparatively low prestige, even though they may involve control over very large resources."[1]

I quote this partly because it is true, partly because it is the situation as it has been up until now. Another point that David Howell underlines very strongly in his article, which is based on first-hand experience inside both the civil service and Marks & Spencer, is that the Civil Service is extremely good on paper, extremely good on presenting arguments to ministers, on helping them, and briefing them for their performance as ministers – not so good in terms of the characteristic management skills as seen in industry.

And this of course in connected with the point mentioned in chapter 1 that our method of government is a Cabinet system responsible for many different departments. Agreement has to be reached between these several departments. Consultation, and ultimately compromise, is one of the orders of the day; not for dishonourable reasons, but for the sheer need to accommodate the various interests of the several ministers and the several departments concerned. So there has to be a great deal of consultation, compromise and paper-based skills.

There is a continuing debate about the need for and effectiveness of these skills. It is typified on the one hand by John Garrett, a former Labour MP and a member of the Fulton Committee, complaining about the absence of management type skills in the Civil Service, and saying that it is absurd that the Civil Service does not develop those hard-edged, quantitative managerial skills that one finds in the private sector; and on the other hand by a spokesman for the Civil Service position, such as Sir Kenneth Clucas, a highly thoughtful, ex-permanent secretary, who argues that these skills that I have described, the ability to be good on paper, to compromise, to consult, to advise ministers and so on, are the skills that go with working in a parliamentary system. If your minister has to go down to the House of Commons to answer some difficult and perhaps unanswerable point, you as a civil servant have to be able to brief him or her in a way that will enable them to do just that. The skills that are valued, argues Sir Kenneth, and will continue to be needed while we have a parliament-based system, are those that go with parliamentary accountability. That briefly is the background to and the nature of the career, together with some of the influences that shape it, but we must be wary all the time of over-generalising.

Values and Attitudes

But what influences how our top policy makers look at the world and the kind of approach they bring to dealing with problems? It cannot be emphasised too strongly the plus side, at least at the very top, of the strong and honourable sense of what one might call "the public service obligation", the expectation that this is a lifetime career. It is summed up in the view: "I have come into this at 23. I expect to stay till I am 60. I shall not abandon ship if I don't like it or the going is too rough." There is a sense, based on the 19th century empire building tradition, that here is an obligation that a young man or woman takes on and maintains throughout a lifetime. It is extremely important. It is a disinterested and unself-serving profession in marked contrast to bureaucracies elsewhere and, I would suggest, in contrast with some parts of the bureaucracy even in this country. There is a strong sense of pride in the profession; a strong emphasis on the informal rules, indeed a belief that formal rules are unnecessary. There is for instance great disgust felt by many civil servants at unauthorised leaks. This is outside the formal and indeed the informal rules of behaviour – not how one should behave even if one disapproves of what one's Minister or the government as a whole might be doing. Above all, there is the insistence that the good civil servant is not only obliged but able to serve any minister of any party, impartially and loyally; and that within that framework the job of the civil servant is not to make policy, but to advise ministers on making policy and then to implement their decisions. Many civil servants are extremely reluctant to accept the point of view that they in some sense make policy simply by giving certain advice to ministers. Many outside critics on the other hand say that it is inherent in an organisation whose members work for a long time in a particular context and live with certain sorts of policies that they, even unconsciously, make rather than simply implement policy.

In terms of values and attitudes towards the profession of the Civil Service as a career things may be changing. I am sure that attitudes differ as between the senior and the junior grades. Another comment from David Howell:

"The gap between the centre and the field is far wider in the civil service than in Marks & Spencer and levels of motivation are lower. Motivation is probably highest near the top and in those further flung parts of the service where the tasks are stable, reasonably rewarded and generally recognised to be necessary. But elsewhere levels of satisfaction and motivation are much lower, reflecting the changes in composition and outlook which have taken place, especially in departments with large local office networks. Compared to the pre-war period, or even to the 1950s, today's civil service is younger, less stable and committed, and less motivated by the ethic of public service."[2]

The growing militancy of the civil service trade unions has been seen already, culminating in the strike in 1982. It is interesting that when I asked two groups of new graduates totalling about 60 young administration trainees who had recently joined the Civil Service whether they regarded the Civil Service as a lifetime career, 54 said that they did not regard it necessarily as a lifetime career. I think that this may be the changing view of new entrants towards the Civil Service as a profession. This factor is something which industrialists and others may need to consider in thinking about Whitehall and their dealings with the Civil Service.

With the lifetime career and the kind of background that I have mentioned goes a very strong belief in the importance of good and orderly government; and a fear sometimes that outside intervention may impede this. It is a fear which partly underlies the secretiveness of Whitehall – a belief that the outsider often has nothing to contribute except trouble and half-baked ideas and hence a reticence to discuss new ideas publicly. Linked with this is too often a scepticism about first, the feasibility, and secondly, the likely net benefit of major change. This is reinforced by the reasonable thought that those who advocate such changes, that is very often Ministers, often have not thought through all the implications of the new proposals. Change is frequently introduced for political reasons. And, what is more, the same minister, will often not still be in post to pick up the pieces when something goes catastrophically wrong. It is not just civil servants who move rapidly from job to job, ministers do as well. Most civil servants because they work in the one department will therefore have to deal with the problems left over from well-intentioned policies which have gone wrong. These problems combine with and help to reinforce a civil service attitude towards politicians which is at best detached. This detachment goes with the civil service career, a career which does not bring them socially and privately into contact with the political groups, any more than it brings civil servants socially and privately into contact with the commercial and industrial sector. I say it leads to an attitude towards politicians which is at best detached. At worst it is sometimes hostile. There is a real problem about the gap between the political and the bureaucratic cultures. The two worlds work closely on government, but do not understand or relate to each other nearly as well as they should. This helps to explain some of the relationships with ministers that one has seen portrayed in the television series *Yes, Minister* – loyal, though sometimes exasperated; polite, but often indifferent; and a relationship which can often be surprisingly formal. Civil servants are anxious to do what ministers want if it makes sense – but all too often they find that in their view a political judgement does not make sense and they cannot see that it could make sense.

Civil servants are not anxious to control ministers but are glad to follow a strong lead. They respect and enjoy working for the Denis Healeys, the Michael Heseltines, or the Nigel Lawsons as people who will go into Cabinet and push their departmental point of view forward. This is appreciated by civil servants in departments, who want above all a minister who will do his job as a departmental minister; but they are always very conscious in relation to ministers in particular, first, that they will have to do the dirty work, to sort out the mess if things go wrong and, secondly, that it is they who will have to advise on solutions if things go wrong.

This concern of civil servants, together with the separateness of the world of politicians and the world of civil servants, can lead to the existence of civil service policies or rather "departmental policies" which are not necessarily those of their ministers. Civil servants certainly try to point out to ministers the consequences of what they see as unwise actions or foolish proposals, and to dissuade them from doing things that they see as being foolish. They also see it as their job to protect what they regard as the national interest. But if you are a civil servant working in the Department of Trade and Industry or the Home Office, what you see as the national interest will tend to be that bit of the community, and that bit of the national activity for which you are responsible.

It is important not to forget how fragmented Whitehall is and that the word itself is a convenient label to cover an extraordinary variety of departments, not only in size but also in terms of style and outlook. The Home Office is light years away in the way in which it views the world from the Department of Trade and Industry; the Department of Education and Science is very different from the Department of the Environment. That is the point made earlier. Most people in departments work their lifetime within that department. The distinctive culture of the department is at least as important as the culture of Whitehall as a whole. There is no doubt in my mind, based on my own brief period in the Department of Industry under labour ministers, that there was considerable reluctance on the part of the department – to use a collective noun – to implement to the hilt some of the things that labour ministers were trying to do in relation to industrial policy because, as the department saw it and as the department's clients saw it, these policies would damage the private sector of industry. To that extent, while there was no disloyalty, there was considerable reluctance and unease about some of the things – for example, planning agreements – which were part of the established and accepted policy of the government of the day. Similarly there will be reluctance on the part of civil servants in the Department of the Environment engaged as some would see it on a headlong flight to catastrophe as far as local government is concerned, to implement some of the policies of Michael Heseltine or Patrick Jenkin, or on the part of some civil servants in the Department of Health and Social Security with regard to changes being introduced in the Health Service. Certainly there is a desire to protect that bit of the national interest for which they are professionally responsible – local government, the private sector of industry, the health service – and to dissuade their ministers from doing foolish and damaging things.

All these factors, plus the sheer complexity of the organisation at Whitehall and the difficulty of securing agreement between those different departments headed by their different ministers, and sometimes chaired by a Prime Minister who may not always know what he or she wants to do, lead to a reluctance to implement ill-considered change which can slop over into reluctance to implement change at all. The detachment that goes with loyalty to governments of either party, the knowledge that you will have to be willing, as a top civil servant, to advise a Conservative Government in this quinquennium and perhaps a Labour Government in the next, does mean, as a celebrated civil service lecture given by a senior civil servant has put it, that you have to withhold the last 5% of commitment – a point which was picked up very angrily by Sir John Hoskyns in one of his talks, commenting that this was not the approach for a Civil Service which was required to help bring about a series of major changes in a nation in a state of continuing crisis. Based on my own experience partly in a department, but more particularly looking at the problem from the centre, which gives one a different perhaps misleading perspective, I would say that one can come across a sense of pessimism about what can be done, and here the Hoskyns' phrase is at least a starting point for debate:

"Few, if any, civil servants believe that the country can be saved."[3]

Again that goes back to the belief that it has all been tried before – as very often it has; the belief that politicians all too often do not know what they are doing – sometimes justified; and the belief that there tends to be, at least in a political system, an ill-controlled, unplanned, but politically necessary oscillation between different sorts of policies in response to popular demands, changes of administration and the consequent redefining of priorities.

When Sir John Hoskyns was asked on television what his single change would be in the Civil Service if he had to make it, he replied off the cuff that he would compulsorily retire everybody over 50. I think that is foolish. If I had to suggest a single change or set of changes, I would try to encourage movement in all directions, permanent and temporary, between the private sector and the civil service as a career move; people coming in and staying in; people coming in on secondment; people going out permanently if they get bored, tired, burnt out, or find that their skills lie elsewhere; people going out on secondment on a much larger scale than at present. What is more, movement within the public sector; people moving between the Department of Health and Social Security and, for instance, the Health Service. You can count the numbers of such movements on one hand; and people moving between the Department of the Environment and local government where you can count the number of movements on half a hand. Finally, I would advocate movement within the Civil Service itself, between the industry departments and the welfare departments; between the Department of Education and Science and the Department of Defence. There are skills and techniques which are just as relevant in one department, for all that its subject matter is different, as in another. These movements would help to break down some of that sense of departmental particularism and those sometimes rather rigid departmental cultures, which are so much part of the fragmentation of Whitehall.

Notes

1. *Public Administration* Volume 59, 1981, p.348.
2. *Ibid.*
3. Sir John Hoskyns, *Westminster and Whitehall: an Outsider's View*. Speech to the annual dinner of the Institute of Fiscal Studies, October 1982.

3

RECENT DEVELOPMENTS

PETER LE CHEMINANT CB

To begin by defining terms. I am discussing the Home Civil Service, not the National Health Service nor local government. Nor am I discussing the nationalised industries; the Civil Service has financial and other relationships with them but it does not manage them.

In the first two chapters the discussion has been mostly of relationships at the policy level. This chapter is concerned with the manpower of the Home Civil Service as a whole. There are about 617,000 civil servants organised in some 30 government departments, working in about 10,000 establishments, offices and centres scattered throughout the country. Looking at all these places and people, it is important to remember that in terms of manpower – which is our biggest resource – the overwhelming majority of civil servants (some 80%) do only four things. They collect taxes, they pay benefits ranging from retirement pensions to regional development grants, they support the armed forces, and they contribute to law and order by running the courts and guarding the prisons. For every Permanent Secretary – the archetypal civil servant – we employ six pyschologists; 12 factory inspectors; 14 prison governors; 15 photographers; 16 medical doctors; 20 economists and statisticians; 25 agricultural workers; 26 bailiffs; 37 custom officers; 50 professional valuers; 100 policemen – our own not the Metropolitan; 100 personal secretaries; 158 tax inspectors; 200 data processors; 400 prison officers; 400 scientists; 1,000 engineers and technicians; well over 3,000 blue-collar workers of all kinds; and some 10,000 assorted clerks, astro-physicists, typists, patent examiners and so on. We have over 3,000 different trades, ranks and grades in the Service. There are a lot of people doing a lot of very different things. It is a long way from the TV world of *Yes, Minister* and it is a long way indeed, for the most part, from "policy".

What the Service is doing therefore is running a complex and diverse series of businesses, outputs of which range from collecting many tens of billions of taxes a year, through paying over 9 million retirement pensions every week, to catching a thousand drug smugglers a year, guarding about 45,000 involuntary guests in Her Majesty's prisons, and manufacturing weapons of all types including nuclear weapons. Policy is naturally part of the scene, but from the point of view of managing this great organisation it is a relatively small part.

All of this is expensive to run. Excluding the armed forces, the total civil service wage bill, including national insurance contributions, overtime, etc., is about £5 billion a year. Other administrative expenses, including capital expenditure and the notional rent paid for service owned buildings amount to about a further £11 billion a year. It is a lot of money. The rest of public expenditure – figures are mentioned well in excess of £100 billion – is for the most part what is called "programme expenditure". It comprises such things as £15 billion for retirement pensions; £2 billion for unemployment benefit; £16 billion for other forms of social security; £14 billion passed on to local authorities and so on. The cost of running the Civil Service is about 12% of the total costs of government, all the rest of government expenditure goes to other people in one way or another.

All of this expenditure has to be paid for. Yet government has no money; anything they spend they get from taxes or through borrowing. In 1984/85 they aimed to raise about £32 billion from income tax, £17 billion from national insurance contributions, and so on. Very big numbers.

It is clear then that the taxpayer is entitled to ask several questions. How good is the Service at running these businesses, undertaking the management task? What is being done to improve performance so as to get better value for money? These are very fair initial questions. A further question is what is being done to get better value for money from the programme expenditure which is overwhelmingly the major part of government expenditure? In addition to the management questions and the value for money questions, businessmen would also expect to ask what direct effects do civil service activities have on industry bearing in mind that taxes are part of industry's expenditure and that government purchases, loans and grants are either industry's income or the income of its customers? The final question is what indirect knock-on effects do civil service management activities have on industry, for example in the labour market? The Civil Service recruits about 30,000 people a year from all sorts of educational backgrounds and with a wide variety of skills. When addressing these questions it is important to realise that the answers to them involve the activities of both civil servants and ministers.

How good is the Civil Service at its job of managing its executive functions? It is not possible to answer in any absolute or total sense. Clearly there is one level at which it succeeds: retirement pensions, unemployment benefit and such things do get paid, and by and large paid on time. Large numbers of the unemployed find work through our Job Centres. Driving licences get issued; task forces are sent to the Falklands – and the Civil Service had a fair hand in that. The courts do operate and most of our convicts stay behind bars. Whether we succeed in all this at minimal cost or through obtaining maximum value for money – they are not necessarily the same thing – is another matter. This is the point where Civil Service experience and industry's experience tends to diverge. The businessman in one sense is very lucky in that he has a very simple test of success: the bottom line on the balance sheet. The Civil Service does not have that luxury. Of course there are wide areas where unit costs are measured, for example in the paying of pensions, or the output achieved with given resources, for example student days per teacher at the Civil Service College. But large parts of its output are not measurable in money terms. How can the value of providing a better tank be measured? Or the value of improving the services or shortening the queues at a social security office? Indeed how do you measure the value of reducing the number of errors made in tax assessments?

But the Civil Service has tried to perform its job efficiently. It has absorbed – since before 1979 – successive cuts in manpower and money and still manages to keep the service rolling. The public service is of course unable to drop unprofitable tasks. It now places much more emphasis on management experience and expertise in the career development of staff. They are better trained and have all learnt quite a bit in the hard school of experience. New techniques and systems are being introduced all the time, but the most important event of the last few years has been the development of the Financial Management Initiative (FMI). For the first time ever, financial management techniques have been developed for use in the Civil Service, representing a further step on the road to a systematic reappraisal of activities and – this is very important – to a devolution of responsibility. The current theme at every level in the Civil Service is to find out who does what, why they do it, what they achieve and what it costs. The idea is not only to clarify objectives. Output is being measured as far as possible, and the system has produced a very much better flow of internal financial management information than ever before. There is no doubt whatever that a few years ago there was plenty of information for senior staff at departmental level, connected with the work of the department as a whole. There was however a very real dearth of financial information about what specific operations actually cost, or any breakdown of those costs. We are now seeking to put that right. In the case of the Cabinet Office (Management and Personnel Office) progress is being made. We have a new computer system which came on-line in Spring 1984 and which now indicates what every different part of the department spends on its salaries, postage, travel and subsistence, or, even, buying cups of tea for visitors.

The Financial Management Initiative is not the whole story. There are many other aspects to this control. The most publicly visible are the scrutiny technique associated with Lord Rayner which, over the last few years, have led to a systematic look at specific sections of the government's work. The great thing about the Rayner scrutiny techniques is that no holds are barred and parts of the operation have been looked at in an iconoclastic way, calling attention to relationships, costs, current methods and possible alternatives which would not otherwise have come to light.

Parliament, too, has helped a great deal. The development since 1979 of Departmental Select Committees, within which MPs concentrate on the affairs of one department, is yielding a volume of information and informed comment which is at the heart of reform.[1] It is beneficial that Parliament knows more about the activities of the Civil Service and this can be better achieved through departmental contact with Parliament than simply by ministers answering parliamentary questions and debates.

But more is involved than simply shedding functions or cutting costs; obtaining value for money can sometimes mean spending some to save some – a proposition which runs hard up against Treasury doctrines of yearly accounting which means that if you do not spend your vote this year the money returns to the Exchequer.

Let me give an example of a change introduced in my last job, when I was in the Treasury in charge of Civil Service pay. For the sake of efficiency it was decided that weekly paid staff should be paid monthly. Because of their contracts of service they could not be forced to move to monthly pay by credit transfer, so they were offered £100 a head to switch. So far, three-quarters of the non-industrial weekly paid staff – we cannot touch the industrials because of the Truck Acts – have changed and the cost saving recouped the £100 within a twelve-month.

I have talked above about programme expenditure. Much of it is the transfer of cash acquired from taxpayers in general to individuals or to companies, and the transfer of cash to other organisations such as the NHS or local authorities, which themselves use it for a multitude of purposes. Some of it is capital expenditure on roads and military hardware of various kinds. I have mentioned problems of improvements in assessing value for money in the Civil Service's own domestic operations. The problem of assessing value for money in the wider area of programme expenditure for which the Civil Service is responsible is very great indeed. How much better off is the nation as a whole if the government takes money from tax payers and gives it to a group of individuals, a company, a local authority, etc? These are areas where nobody has yet found a satisfactory technical answer, cost benefit analysis of the old kind notwithstanding. They are also of course areas with considerable political implications.

The third category of questions set out earlier concerns the direct effects of civil service activities on the business community. This also takes us to the heart of politics. An old politician once said, "politics is about 'oo gets wot." It is a good working definition. Ministers decide to tax the population in various ways, and then decide to spend the money in various ways. Civil servants are the instruments through which they give effect to their decisions. They are also a source of policy advice to Ministers. But they do not tell them what to do. There are plenty of people around, including lobbies, companies and associations, who are ready, willing and able to do that. The civil servant's job fundamentally is to say, "If you want to achieve X, then the options are Y and the costs and consequences are Z." Some years ago a senior civil servant shortly after his retirement was asked by an interviewer whether he had felt frustrated when ministers did not take his advice, and he said, "No, not at all. If I'd wanted to be a minister I'd have gone into politics." The second is a remark by a wise old deputy secretary who was overheard saying to his minister one day, "You're the boss, you carry the can, but don't say afterwards I didn't warn you." To my mind that is the perfect description of the relationship between policy civil servants and their ministers. It is a very interesting relationship, but again it is a long way from the working conditions set out in *Yes, Minister*.

The final question was, what are the indirect knock-on effects of what the Civil Service does? There are many of these but I will mention just a few. If the attempt to get a tougher, more managerially aware, more cost-conscious Civil Service is successful, then that will do one thing which must be good – it will reduce the tax burden. But it will have other effects. The Service will become much tougher when it comes to buying goods. Already it is a long way from cost plus, but has not yet quite achieved the relationship of a Marks & Spencer and its suppliers; but given the great volume of government purchases, that day may come. Civil service managers now know that their prospects are on the line, for the management of resources as well as systems. When they look at their accounts in detail they will be asking questions of a kind which they would not have thought about a year or two ago, or certainly four or five years ago. A number of the relationships and assumptions which currently exist throughout society, for example where government is involved with industry, may well begin to slip a little when the new machinery starts automatically to print out the costs of various policy decisions. There will be further changes by asking questions – "What is the objective? What are we achieving? What does it cost? How does it measure up against other things? Is there a better way?" On the labour front too, industrialists must expect more competition. In one sense we have always had to compete but at the margin the competition becomes more intense; and in all large organisations such as the Civil Service, which recruit significant numbers of scarce specialists, the margin can be quite large.

Throughout the scrutiny programmes and the Financial Management Initiative run the questions: do we need to undertake function X at all? If we do what is the most effective way of doing it? In a sense the FMI is a massive liberation of the latent commercial instincts at all management levels in the Civil Service. There will be a lot of enthusiasts rushing around, trying to make sure their budgets are met, once they are properly established. This is welcome from the tax point of view more particularly when work is passed on which certainly can be done more cheaply through private enterprise. Privatisation is already taking place. The most recent example in my own department was only a few weeks ago when we decided that it was cheaper to buy in our press cuttings from a press cuttings service than to have a couple of our clerks preparing them. We do not save much money in the short run, but we pay no national insurance, have no pension obligations, and altogether it is better once you have got through the problems of actually getting it started. To take another instance, we have recently put out to contract the catering services of the Civil Service College in Sunningdale. A great deal of work is bound to be transferred as we compare costs and values both internally and externally and then go for the better buy.

Clarifying objectives, performance and costs will make civil servants lives more exciting, but they will also have profound implications for Ministers. The days of the amateur are over for them as well as for their civil servants: it will be interesting to see where that fact leads. Relationships between the Government – ministers and civil servants – and Parliament are also changing. MPs too are much more professional than they used to be, and the new Departmental Select Committees are providing them with a day to day entrée into the workings of government creating a greater understanding of the real problems which face everyone, parliamentarians, ministers, civil servants or anybody else. Select Committee reports tend mostly to be free from the party stances and attitudes which are part of set piece debates in the House of Commons on a specific issue. If MPs tackle a problem with some reasonable professional advisers at their elbow, and a good ongoing dialogue with ministers and officials in a department, they can make coherent and worthwhile reports. I shall know that the system has finally worked when we get a report from a Select Committee which says, "We've had a look at this problem and by and large we think the Government have got it about right." Perhaps that day will never come!

Recruitment to the Civil Service is a large and complicated subject and two recent developments should be mentioned. Over the last few years the upper age limits have been removed in recruitment competitions, and now 90% of the applicants for Civil Service jobs when they are advertised can be of almost any age. More mature recruitment is undertaken than used to be the case. Of course there are many specialist grades where recruitment at mature ages has always been, and remains, a feature of life. There is also a practice of recruiting people in mid-career, in their 30s and 40s, direct from industry and elsewhere at senior administrative (Principal) level. These recruits bring qualities and experience that we felt the Civil Service needed and they have been very successful. There was a break in these competitions through the period of staff reductions, recruitment bans and so on, but in the autumn of 1983 it was reinstated in a limited way and may be used again as circumstances require.

In conclusion the change in title from the Management and Personnel Office to the Cabinet Office (Management and Personnel Office) has an importance which may not be fully appreciated outside the Service. Links had always been strong with the Cabinet Office but the new arrangements mean it is now formally a part of the Cabinet Office in the centre of Whitehall – sharing facilities, staff and so on. Most of the London staff have moved into the same building as the Treasury. Add to that the fact that the Minister for the Civil Service is the Rt. Hon. Mrs. Margaret Thatcher and it is clear that the central personnel function is back at the heart of Whitehall's affairs.

Note

1. For comments on and details of the work of these Departmental Select Committees during their first Parliament 1979-1983 see *Commons Select Committees: Catalysts for Progress*? edited by Dermot Englefield, Longman, 1984.

4

TRAINING FOR THE FUTURE

DENNIS TREVELYAN CB

The first thing to say about training in the Civil Service is that it supports an organisation that is large and varied. Civil servants have little in common beyond their name and employer, and it makes no sense to think of a single training and career development pattern for all staff: the responsibility for ensuring that people are properly trained rests with the department in which they are employed. You will find warship designers who are civil servants, coastguards and even bee-keepers. Even though the Civil Service has contracted substantially since 1979 and many former civil servants' tasks are now undertaken by the private sector, there are still few trades or professions that are not employed in it somewhere. And all of these people need appropriate training.

To train staff to deal with all this calls for effort and staff training is big business. About £170 million (including the cost of student time) was spent on it in 1983, providing some 25,000 courses for around 300,000 civil servants. The Civil Service spends as much on training as good outside employers – about 4% of the payroll – but this is still less than ten years or so ago when there was something of a surge following publication of the Fulton Report. Naturally, training has not been exempt from recent pressures to reduce costs and to increase efficiency, and one of the recurring themes in advice to training managers is that they must clearly identify costs so that better decisions about training can be made. The point is that training is only justified by the contribution it makes towards improving efficiency and effectiveness; there has to be a continual re-appraisal of emphasis and priorities in order to give the best return on the training investment.

Three quarters of all Civil Service training is run by the departments, just as three quarters is for junior or middle-grade staff. The exact way in which this training is organised depends on the structure and role of individual departments, but all are required to appoint a Departmental Training Officer to manage the training plan and to act as a link to the Cabinet Office (Management and

Personnel Office) Training Division who have general oversight of Civil Service training and who provide a support and consultancy service for departments. Also, the Civil Service College is an important unit within the Cabinet Office. Departments have their own training resources (altogether there are some 3000 staff working full time in the training field) but they also make much use of outside experts – both by contracting out (sending staff off to be trained) and by buying in (using consultants to run in-house courses). About 20% of Civil Service training is provided externally.

The Civil Service spent £28 million (again including the cost of student time) on sending 33,000 civil servants off to courses or seminars at external institutions last year. They ranged from those reading for higher level degrees to those attending a one-day seminar. The Business Schools, Management Colleges, Regional Management Centres, Colleges of Further Education, the Universities, and training courses run by major companies, are used as well as a range of specialist training institutions. Contacts with the private sector, with academics, and with other managers in the public sector are also valued, because the interchange of ideas and experience is an important training ingredient. External training is being used more. We are also trying to introduce more joint training ventures with private sector employers; these add to interchange of expertise.

Apart from the training in departments and external training, the Civil Service College provides for about 4% of the total. The College does not compete with departments: rather the two should be seen as one single complementary in-house training organisation, with the College providing that which is most effectively carried out centrally. Last year around 20,000 civil servants attended courses at, or organised by, the College – most took place in its residential centre at Sunningdale or its non-residential centre in London, but some were run in various parts of the country either in departments or in other institutions under special sponsorship arrangements. The College does not exist solely or mainly for an elite of "high fliers" although naturally it attracts people who are expected to go further in their careers. Students range from Clerical Officer to Permanent Secretary, and they come from all disciplines – statisticians, economists, lawyers, doctors, scientists and engineers as well as general administrators. Very little of the training is mandatory, and departments are under no obligation to use the College at all. They pick courses there for students in the same way as they consider outside options – and although at present some developmental courses are paid for centrally, from April 1986 there will be a staged move to a situation where all courses are charged for directly. This may sharpen comparisons with external practice, and make the College even more responsive to the requirements of line managers in departments.

The College has about 100 teaching staff, who come from universities, polytechnics, industry, commerce and from other government departments. The last category, who come to the College on loan for about 4 years, will have first-hand experience of the subjects they teach, for example computers, economics and policy formulation. About half the teaching sessions are given by outsiders. The list of speakers is by any standards impressive, and includes Ministers, MPs, prominent academics, journalists and political commentators, trade unionists and top executives from both public and private sectors.

About 80% of civil service training is for fairly junior staff to train them to carry out a specific task; of the remainder, 14% of training is devoted to managers and supervisors and the rest to induction training (to introduce people to a new part of the organisation or to a new grade). The basic pattern of training was set in 1974 when the Civil Service introduced a series of "frameworks" to guide the training of staff up to the Senior Executive Officer grade. The frameworks were a basis for further innovation; by and large they still stand. But it is essential to take account of developments arising from a changing approach both to vocational training and to education, and of those arising from changes in society itself. The impact of changing work patterns, as technology makes itself felt more and more, reinforces the inevitability of change in the way in which the training of junior and middle-grade staff is structured.

In addition, it is important to give weight to the development and training for senior managers in the Civil Service. Senior civil servants – that is, the top six grades, have had training in the past. But more needs to be done, especially for those at the top or likely to get there. In the past the Civil Service has gone to a lot of trouble to attract the best people, the "alpha minds" of chapter 11, into the key areas. And in the past overwhelming attention at senior levels has been focused on the formulation of policy and less on management generally. But as government has grappled with more complex issues and as the resources managed by departments have become more constrained, so managerial problems have grown too. Good and effective management of a department is essential and civil service managers have responded. Much of this flows from measures introduced by the present Administration, most critically those initiatives which give individual managers clear objectives and plainly stated resource allocations for their work.

This is well understood by senior civil servants. They have become increasingly aware of the need to improve skills and knowledge in certain critical areas; an increase in take up on College courses, especially by senior staff, is testimony to that trend. But more needs to be done and three recent important initiatives seem set to revolutionise Civil Service approach to management development. The first is concerned with identifying and developing junior staff with potential to reach senior grades. The other two focus on preparing people for the most senior posts: the *Top Management Programme* which is a six week course for newly appointed grade 3 (Under Secretary) officers; and the *Senior Management Development Programme* which is being developed both for those likely to reach that grade, and to provide the service with the benefit of greatly improved management in the grades immediately below that level. These three initiatives are of particular significance.

In any effective management system there needs to be a systematic way of dealing with senior staffing. In 1980 the Civil Service introduced better career and succession planning. The prime objective was to identify potential successors for important posts early enough to allow them to be given an appropriate blend of training and experience. Each year departments produce and review a succession plan for every post in the top three grades and for certain other key posts; the plan is based on a profile of requirements for the job and indicates when the post is next expected to be vacated. It identified who could succeed if the post was unexpectedly to be vacated, who would be suitable to succeed in the normal course of events, and who should be in the field for the next-but-one succession. Obviously this system should not be too rigid: the plans are meant as an indicator rather than a blueprint, but they provide a basis on which the careers of individual officers can be planned and developed. It helps departments to identify potential shortages of suitable top managers and it also encourages them to have regular and comprehensive reviews of their senior staffing.

The Civil Service values training contacts with outsiders and recognises the importance of bringing senior, or potentially senior civil servants into personal contact with top leaders and practice in commerce and industry. Many departments already have close relationships with the private sector and find this cross-fertilisation a valuable source of ideas. Secondments and attachments at middle management level and in mid-career are being developed for those who are likely to rise in the service. In 1983, 630 civil servants were sent to outside organisations in this way, but useful secondments are not easy to arrange. There is a limit to the number of opportunities that can be provided; and it is not easy for a receiving organisation to identify a suitably challenging job for someone on loan.

The Civil Service is large and it inevitably faces the formidable problem of how to identify the most talented among staff who are spread across the country and how to balance the development of managers against the routine demands of the service. Part of the answer lies in appraisal systems which are being further refined.

Early in 1984 a series of studies took place across the service to examine ways of bringing on good quality staff at Principal level. The result of these studies is the *Management Development Programme*, a structured and systematic approach to cover the able nominated staff at Executive Officer, Higher Executive Officer and Senior Executive Officer levels. Those involved will be given carefully planned postings to help them develop their potential, and will undertake a programme of formal training related to their work. In general the training will take the form of modular courses, since these fit in far more readily with operational requirements than do long courses; but while there will be central guidelines the detail of the programme will be at the discretion of departments rather than prescribed centrally.

The Senior Management Development Programme arises from our need for a more structured development for those at more senior levels. The most formative of the various factors that combine to develop managers is job experience, whether it is in the department, on loan to another part of government (for example one of the central departments) or on secondment outside the service. Training provides a cruicial supplement. Although the programme will broaden out in due course to involve more staff within the relevant grades, it will concentrate initially on our younger staff: those at Principal level aged under 35, and those at more senior grades aged under 42. But some participants could be older and over a five year period the age limit will be raised each year. Although the programme will not be compulsory – there is an important role for self development – it is expected that staff will see it as a major aid to career progression and take-up will be high. One target will be for all participants to have at least five days training a year and individual logbooks to record progress will be used. A core of "competencies" or "areas of experience" which are likely to be of use to most participants will be defined. Departments and those responsible for specialist functions will do likewise for their own work areas.

The best people in the Civil Service will come through to the Grade 3 level and these have tended in the past to do the least training. To remedy this and to prepare them for the highest ranks, those being promoted to Grade 3 will in future undertake, between jobs, the *Top Management Programme* which will last 6 weeks, for 4 weeks of which the civil servants will be mixed with a similar number of people from the private and other parts of the public sectors. The objectives of the *Programme* are to enable top managers with the highest potential from all sectors of the economy to improve their ability to:-

understand as far as is possible the nature, extent and significance of the fundamental changes taking place in the economic, international, industrial, technological, physical and social environment;

formulate strategies to meet the challenge of those changes and cope with the uncertainties surrounding them, given scarce resources;

seek increased value for money and year-on-year improvements in productivity and efficiency of service to customers, by setting clear objectives and managing organisations and resources positively;

lead and motivate people to carry out tasks efficiently, imaginatively and with commitment;

understand one another's attitudes, priorities and approaches to major problems and issues.

For the civil servant the additional two weeks of the *Programme* will be spent in considering in further depth the challenges facing the civil service in particular in its management of resources and of people; and through a series of options, improving important skills and deepening knowledge of particular subjects.

The *Programme* will be rigorous and demanding but informal and varied, with a strong emphasis on active participation by programme members. Tutors and seminar participants are being drawn from a variety of backgrounds, the common denominator being their high standing in their particular field, be it academic, professional or industrial. A vital part of the *Programme* will be the syndicate work on live problems, rather than historic case studies. A great deal of effort will go into evaluating the *Programme's* quality, the extent to which it meets its objectives and its relevance to the jobs to which the participants will return.

The first three *Programmes* are scheduled to be held in February, July and October 1985, with four a year thereafter. Each will cater for 24 participants, about 10 civil servants at or around the point of promotion to Under Secretary (Grade 3) two or three from local authorities and other government bodies, about three from the nationalised industries and some nine from private sector companies.

Training in the Civil Service, and for that matter elsewhere, is not an end in itself; nor can it be considered in isolation since it is only one aspect, although a very important one, of management development of staff. There are two main reasons why training in the Civil Service is now so important. The first is that at a time when there have been reductions in manpower and tight budgetary constraints, the Civil Service, like other organisations, must develop and use to the full the talents and abilities of staff. Effective management, in the sense of good house-keeping, is important at all levels so that a proper and economic service is given to ministers, Parliament and the general public. Management development to enable staff to have the appropriate experience and knowledge to do their jobs properly is, therefore, essential and in any programme to achieve better results training must provide an essential part.

But there is a second and more important reason. The Civil Service, like other large-scale organisations, faces a new world. The nature of public business becomes increasingly more complex; the international dimension obtrudes more and more on domestic concerns; the machinery of management, with its increasing reliance on new technologies, demands more of the manager; and the battery of techniques and skills which a manager has to possess are now formidable. The content of civil service work is increasingly more managerial in nature although policy work, insofar as it can be distinguished, is no less demanding. The reaction of the Civil Service to this changing work environment is to place more emphasis on explicit statements of targets and objectives; and there is an enhanced degree of delegated management and this places new demands on staff at every level. Over the years recruits to the Civil Service have been people of considerable intellectual and personal calibre – the entry qualifications and care with which recruitment is conducted attest to this – but they too will need help to prepare themselves for the challenges of the 1990s. The training programmes which this chapter describes are an attempt to gear the Civil Service to meet those challenges.

2

THE CIVIL SERVICE AND PARLIAMENT

Chapter 5

The Role of the Minister
Charles Morris

Chapter 6

Accountability to Parliament
The Rt. Hon. Sir Edward du Cann

Chapter 7

Information for Parliament
Dermot Englefield

5

THE ROLE OF THE MINISTER

CHARLES MORRIS

In Part 1 of the book we have been considering the Civil Service per se. Throughout these chapters there have been references to Parliament. The next three chapters consider the work of the Civil Service in relation to the work of Parliament, the role of which is to legislate and subject the government's proposals and performance to continuing examination.

The key figure in this relationship is the minister whose responsibilities are both within his department and also directly and personally to Parliament. He is the bridge joining the executive and the legislature; hence this chapter is in two parts, namely the minister in his department, discussing as an example the minister for the Civil Service, and then the minister in Parliament.

The Minister in his Department

Constitutionally the Prime Minister is the Minister for the Civil Service. Her official designation is Prime Minister, First Lord of the Treasury and Minister for the Civil Service. In recent years, however, ministerial responsibility for the day to day management of the Civil Service was devolved first to the Lord Privy Seal, supported by a Minister of State operating within a separate and independent Civil Service Department and then came what many regarded as the inexplicable decision taken by the present administration to roll back the recommendations of the Fulton Committee, abolish the Civil Service Department, and transfer its functions back from whence they came – to the Treasury. In mid-1984 ministerial responsibility for civil service manpower, pay and pensions, is carried by the Minister of State at the Treasury, Mr. Hayhoe, who, incidentally, answers for the Civil Service in the House of Commons. Sir Robin Ibbs advises the Prime Minister on efficiency, whilst responsibility for civil service management and personnel policies is with a Treasury spokesman in the House of Lords, the Earl of Gowrie, perhaps better known as the Minister for the Arts. Those with a somewhat cynical turn of mind may well conclude that in a Britain where the civil servant has brought the practice of government administration to the level of an art form, a knowledge of the arts may, perhaps, be a fitting attribute for a minister to bring to the task of managing the Civil Service!

I believe it is the critically important area of civil service management which will, and rightly should, command the attention of any minister with responsibility for the Civil Service. Increasingly, administrative decisions by the Civil Service touch the lives of everyone particularly at a time which has seen a subtle, but significant, change in peoples' perception of the power of government to influence not only the world in which Britain exists, but also to determine the total economic, social, and environmental framework in which we live out our lives. Increased demands for greater government and ministerial intervention, the growth of pressure group politics, and the problems associated with politically rising expectations, are all reflections of this change in peoples' attitudes.

There are, inevitably, numerous claims on the time of the minister with responsibility for the Civil Service. But his primary political role is to effect the implementation of any specific policy commitments which the government, of which he is a member, may have in relation to the Civil Service and its work. He also, of course, carries the responsibility for the staffing, work inspection and work measurement standards, which together with career development procedures, are common to the Civil Service as a whole. Additionally, the minister seeks to ensure that the resources available for both the training and promotion of the efficiency of the Civil Service are adequate to maintain a high level of administrative efficiency in responding to the political direction of ministers and also the changing political and parliamentary environment in which policy is formulated. It is an interesting, indeed, fascinating, feature of the british system of government administration that, given the intense and, at times, agonising controversy surrounding the formulation of policy within individual political parties, the detailed interpretation and legislative framework of policy is almost exclusively entrusted by ministers to a Civil Service which seeks to operate without overt political commitment.

The policy formulation process within government administration proceeds at a number of levels. Immediately a general election is under way the Civil Service prepares policy position papers on the basis of manifestos prepared by the individual political parties fighting the election. Consequently, irrespective of which party wins, policy options have been identified, ready for consideration and implementation by the incoming government, and thus the continuity of civil service administration is maintained. The initiation of new policies and changes in existing ones may come from ministers reacting to parliamentary and political pressures. But it is equally and, perhaps, more likely to emerge from the work of the network of cabinet sub-committees to which policy proposals are referred prior to submission to the cabinet. Policy formulation also proceeds, of course, in that intensely sensitive area, the interface between ministers and their senior civil service advisers.

In recent years politicians have proved themselves positively forthcoming in giving their interpretations of the influence exerted by civil servants on policy formulation. Allegations have been made that civil servants "bounce" ministers into making decisions: that the Civil Service is guilty of what might be termed administrative inertia when processing a policy with which it disagrees, and that it indulges in manipulating ministers by isolating and restricting access to them, thereby making them dependent on the Whitehall machine. It would be misleading to make the assumption that inside every Permanent Secretary is a politician fighting to get out. Nor are ministers and their civil service advisers locked into a world of constant political creative tension. But the light which these allegations throw on minister – civil servant relationship, and the certainty with which former ministers have made the charges, merit examination.

Turning first to the charge that, on occasions, civil servants "bounce" ministers into making decisions. This could, of course, be the understandable reaction to a minister who, having been pressurised by his civil servants to make a decision, subsequently finds it to have been the wrong one. After all, I have never heard of a minister complaining that he was "bounced" into making the right decision! But, given the pressures to which ministers are now subject, including their increasing accountability to the electorate via radio, TV, and the press, it is not unreasonable to demand adequate time to make a considered judgment on the matters which come before them for decision. Equally, it must be said that to a minister eager to get his policy moving, to have to listen to earnest civil servants patiently explaining that collective ministerial accountability involves co-ordinating the response to any policy initiative with all ministers who have a departmental interest in the subject must sound and seem, awfully like administrative inertia.

In politics there are few more exhilarating moments than when the Prime Minister invites you to assume ministerial responsibility. It is only when you arrive at your department and find yourself surrounded by able and administratively competent civil servants with whom you have no shared political commitment, and who defy political identity, that ministerial political isolation takes on a real significance. It cannot be ignored that a departmental Permanent Secretary controlling a ministerial secretariat, with access to the Private Office network, and buttressed by administrators skilled in dealing with ministers, is a formidable influence in policy determination. In the context of the influence exercised by civil servants it is worth remembering the edict heard in the Civil Service Department many years ago "He who writes the minutes makes the policy". The transient nature of ministerial life also poses problems for ministers in their relationship with a permanent Civil Service.

A fascinating insight into the problem of political isolation implicit in the minister-Civil Service relationship is graphically, if somewhat dramatically, illustrated in Barbara Castle's diaries. Highlighting the problems which ministers on occasions experience in seeking to challenge their civil service advisers in departmental policy discussions, she refers to the "sheer pressure" of the official view which, as Secretary of State, she encountered. She writes:

"I thanked God for the allies I have got in the ministerial team, and for the special advisers."[1]

Her reference to special advisers refers, of course, to the politically appointed special advisers instituted under the Harold Wilson administration in 1974. Arguably the interpretation of a minister's political will and intentions is best undertaken by those with a shared political commitment. Yet the absence of any such partiality is of course central to the stance of political neutrality adopted by the civil service. In my view, the solution to the problems associated with the political isolation of ministers within their departments might well lie in adopting the French system of politically appointed ministerial cabinets, which would at least enable ministers to bring a small number of politically sensitive staff into their departments at ministerial Private Office level. I believe an innovation of this nature would reinforce political and ministerial accountability.

The ministerial Private Office is the minister's personal administrative support staff. They are responsible for day-to-day liaison between the minister and his department, for his daily appointments, his diary commitments, and for providing the minister with briefs for ministerial speeches, parliamentary question-time and debates. The Private Office seeks to equip the minister to answer for the administrative and political decisions of his department, and to give effect to the concept of his ministerial accountability to the House of Commons. We tend to overlook the fact that ministerial accountability can and does involve appreciable administrative cost. In a system in which a minister is accountable to the Prime Minister and to parliament, there is an inevitable tendency for the Civil Service to commit to paper and double-bank every phase in the development of policy. This is done for no other reason than to enable individual civil servants to "get from under" if anything should go wrong. Double-banking produces a thousand erudite memos and appended circulation lists with as many as eight names or more, and those cryptic words "to see please". In the world of the policy paper chase within government, initialling these papers is synonymous with endorsement. It is one of those inescapable facts of government administration that, at times of national economic difficulty, rising unemployment, industrial contraction, increasing social distress, the administrative pressures on the Civil Service tend to increase, and the number of civil servants in particular departments rises. But, MP's, who understandably never weary of demanding economies in civil service staffing standards, see no apparent contradiction when they urge simultaneously, greater government intervention and more government provided services and Civil Service manpower cuts.

The Civil Service has been criticised for being too generalist, for having too much influence on policy determination, and lacking in first hand experience of the real world of industry and commerce. Civil service recruitment and selection procedures are controlled, and devised, by the Civil Service Commission, which is independent of government – independent as a result of the Northcote/Trevelyn reforms of 1854–70 which were designed to eliminate political patronage within government administration. Public and parliamentary criticism has largely focused on the selection techniques used for entry to the Administrative Trainee grade – young, graduate, "high fliers". It is argued that the academic background of these recruits tends to be generalist rather than any academic specialism relevant to government administration. The Commission have sought to counter this criticism by arguing that Administrative Trainees are selected on the basis of their intellect and abilities irrespective of the type of academic degree for which they may have studied. It is added that students who study for what might be termed "occupational" degrees, tend to follow their specialism into the relevant professions, and do not see the Civil Service as a first option in assessing their individual career prospects. Anxiety has also been expressed that in the Administrative Trainees' selection interviews, members of the interviewing panels are seeking their "mirror" image, when assessing the candidates who come before them for selection. The Commission has sought to respond to these points by including on the panels conducting the interviews individuals with the requisite qualifications, from the private sector. They also now "trawl" the provincial universities and colleges encouraging undergraduates to seek entry to the Civil Service.

Undoubtedly, given the vagaries of human behaviour, there are individual civil servants who have sought to exercise an undue influence on policy decisions. However, it is also claimed by civil servants that on occasions, in the absence of ministerial direction, or arising from ministerial indecision, circumstances have obliged them to fill what they describe as the "policy vacuum". Without exception, civil servants claim that they respond more effectively to positive ministerial direction and decision.

I believe that government administration must be subject to a continuing process of monitoring and review. It was encouraging to see the decisions to create the post of Parliamentary Commissioner for Administration (the Ombudsman) and to establish Parliamentary Select Committees with a continuing interest in specific Departments of State. Both developments are useful additions to the armoury of surveillance of government administration. It is also contended, probably rightly, that the Civil Service is lacking in first-hand experience and that civil servants, because of the structure of the Service, the promotion processes, and movement within grades, see merely snapshots of industry. They look at industry just for a period of perhaps two or three years. I would like to see the government increasing the existing scheme of secondments to the private sector from the present level of about 140 a year to a figure which has some realistic relationship with the 300 exchanges undertaken within the french and german Civil Services. And one of the achievements of QUANGOs, abolished on specious arguments about "jobs for the boys," was to afford the Civil Service access to useful practical experience.

There are those who believe that the horizons of the individual civil servant can be summed up in three words: pay, pensions and promotion. I am not one of them. I am sad about the crisis of confidence which appears to have afflicted the service in recent years. As a former Minister at the Civil Service Department I have always been impressed with the administrative support and the quality of advice which I have received from the civil service. I found working with civil servants, stimulating, enlightening, challenging, at times positively frustrating, but never dull.

The Minister and Parliament

Some commentators see the House of Commons as a forum in which parliamentarians merely play out the political adversaries game. Such judgements, though understandable, are superficial and ignore the constitutional roles of government and opposition.

The role of government is to govern, to enact legislation, and to account to Parliament for the political and administrative decisions taken collectively by government. Central to the concept of this parliamentary accountability is an obligation carried by prime ministers and ministers to account personally for their policies and their departmental responsibilities direct to the House of Commons. In fact, the very continuance in office of government is wholly and totally dependent on the Prime Minister retaining parliamentary majority support for the government's policies.

Inevitably, Her Majesty's opposition, irrespective of political identity, tend to see their constitutional function and purpose somewhat differently. Whilst there are areas of government policy with which, on occasions, they may agree, the opposition focus their major parliamentary effort on seeking to scrutinise, question, and challenge the actions of government. They also seek to identify and pose alternative policy options for public consideration. In pursuit of these general objectives, the opposition use the whole panoply of parliamentary procedures, to expose the actions of government to the full glare of public attention, and examination.

Perhaps the clearest demonstration of ministerial accountability to Parliament in action, is the hour of parliamentary questions which, Monday to Thursday, precede the scheduled parliamentary business. Questions relevant to a minister's departmental responsibilities are posed on a rota basis, specific days being allocated to individual departments of state. The Prime Minister answers questions for a scheduled fifteen minutes on Tuesday and Thursday afternoons. Answering oral questions in Parliament is very much a spectator sport. As a rule it can be assumed that written parliamentary questions are genuinely seeking a considered and informed answer, whereas the MP who tables an oral parliamentary question usually does so in the knowledge and confident belief that he can predict the initial answer which he is likely to receive. In most cases the purpose of the exercise is to use the tabled oral questions as a vehicle for the supplementary question of which the minister has no prior notice. The uncertainty associated with supplementary questions involves civil servants in appreciable effort in seeking to anticipate and identify all the possible variants to the tabled oral question, which might form the basis of the expected, yet unknown supplementary question. Both the minister and his civil servants are mindful that some seemingly innocuous parliamentary question in the hands of a back-bench MP skilled in exposing the political sensitivities of the government, may well succeed in politically embarrassing the minister and the government which he represents. On one occasion, I enquired of a civil servant as to whether he felt that he had spent a disproportionate amount of time in preparing the ministerial brief for parliamentary questions. He replied "My approach to ministerial accountability is wholly simplistic, and I believe has an inescapable logic. If the minister is obliged to answer to the House of Commons for his responsibilities, I in turn may well be called upon to answer for mine."

It is not always appreciated that the average back-bench MP spends much more of his time listening than speaking. Therefore, irrespective of party political affiliation, many of them quickly acquire a facility for assessing the competence or otherwise of a Minister's "performance". Whilst the House can be quick to react to the pompous, the devious, and the incompetent, invariably, it responds charitably to ministers who, in observing the traditional parliamentary courtesies, openly acknowledge any errors and omissions for which they may have been responsible. Parliamentary courtesy, whilst it may have been designed to take the heat out of political controversy, can also provide verbal pitfalls for the unwary minister. It is an accepted parliamentary courtesy for a minister to address a political opponent as a "honourable gentleman". Equally, he will use the term "honourable friend" in addressing a parliamentary colleague. If, however, the member to whom the minister is addressing his remarks happens to be a Privy Counsellor, then he will expect to be addressed as "right honourable". Parliamentary courtesy also dictates that a member who is a Queen's Counsel may expect to be addressed as "honourable and learned", while a member who has served in the armed services and held the rank of captain or it's equivalent, and above, may be addressed as "honourable and gallant". Happily there is a marked tendency on the part of contemporary parliamentarians to ignore some of the more exaggerated forms of address.

Insofar as public, press, and media interest is focused on the House of Commons, a confident, articulate, minister at ease with his ministerial responsibilities can quickly acquire a national reputation. But, parliamentary exposure can be both an opportunity and a hazard. Whilst some ministers seem positively to blossom in the parliamentary spotlight, others appear to view speaking from the Despatch Box with something less than enthusiasm. It is part of established Westminster folklore that ministerial reputations can be made and lost on the content and presentation of one half-hour ministerial speech. It is also said that a minister is only as good as his last speech. What is undeniable however, is that in defending their political and departmental responsibilities before their fellow parliamentarians, ministers are addressing one of the most politically sophisticated and critical audiences in the land. The incidence of ministerial appearances in the House of Commons can vary markedly dependent on the department of state represented by the individual minister. During the prolonged debates which arise from the presentation of the Budget, Treasury ministers are rarely absent from the chamber of the House of Commons. On the other hand, Foreign Office ministers rarely sponsor specific legislation. Given the added parliamentary obligations to deal with "Private Notice Questions" ministerial "Statements" and at the end of the parliamentary day "Adjournment Debates" plus a commitment to participate in debates and handle legislation appropriate to his department, a minister can, at times, find himself subject to formidable pressures.

His civil servants will ensure that a minister is afforded the maximum administrative support in shouldering his ministerial departmental and also his ministerial parliamentary responsibilities. Equally true however, is the fact that, in keeping with their stance of political neutrality, they will be punctilious in refusing any involvement whatsoever in the minister's party political and constituency commitments.

To achieve political success a minister must seek to balance his administrative, parliamentary, party political, and constituency obligations. He should also endeavour to carry out his ministerial duties in a manner which will reflect favourably on his abilities and to the credit of the government of which he is a member. Prime Ministers who appoint ministers hope for, and expect no less.

Note

1. Barbara Castle, *The Castle Diaries 1974-76*, Wiedenfeld and Nicolson, 1980.

6

ACCOUNTABILITY TO PARLIAMENT

THE RT. HON. SIR EDWARD DU CANN

The House of Commons is in the midst of important constitutional and procedural developments. During the Parliament 1979–1983 stage 1 was successfully accomplished; in the Parliament elected in 1983 we must set our hand to stage 2. It is probably natural that all practical people and indeed the whole of the electorate, are preoccupied with the economy and economic matters. This is not only for the cynical reason that most people judge politics, political parties and politicians by the extent they themselves are affected by what the political parties and the politicians do. Inevitably, people reflect on the balance of payments at one level, interest rates at another, or the level of retirement benefits at a third. "The elevation of the condition of the people", as Mr. Disraeli described it, will always be a paramount aim for politicians. But there is a flip side to the record. Mr. Disraeli spoke also about the upholding of the constitution.

Walking through the Palace of Westminster, I cannot help reflecting how wrong is most people's appreciation of the Houses of Parliament. We see it on *News at Ten* every night. People doing the river trips, tourists and people from the constituencies all say "What a marvellous building!" as foolish a comment, though truthful, as it might be outside a modern factory to say "How nice to work here." Yet, in truth, what do the surroundings matter? Of course one has to provide comfortable circumstances in which people are to work; one is much happier working in a pleasant environment. But what matters in the factory is what the order book is like; how the place is equipped; what is the morale of the people working there; what are the profit margins. It is exactly the same in Parliament. It does not matter in the slightest what the quality of the building is, what matters is how is the work there being done. I have been lucky enough to have been in Parliament for 28 years, but the longer one is there, the more one reflects upon the meaning, the purpose and the intention of the place. I do not believe that Parliament is perfect. You have to work at improving such human institutions the whole time, to examine what they are doing and to check that the place in which they are doing it is in tune with modern circumstances. But I do believe that Parliament, which has provided authority and yet always allowed full discussion, and which broadly speaking over the centuries has kept our nation safe from revolution and serious discord, is in truth a priceless possession.

Quite deliberately, a few years ago, a group of back-bench MPs set out to make a revolution in the way the House of Commons works. Ministers are busy and do not always have time to take the long look that is so often necessary in Parliamentary affairs, so change was promoted by the back-benchers; it has a momentum which remains a powerful one. There is always a dilemma in human circumstances: how to reconcile authority with its control. There is a continuing need to take stock of what Parliament does in the name of us all, because of the amount of constitutional change. Membership of the European Communities will force great changes. There are new party alignments. But apart from obvious things of that sort there are a series of other domestic changes which, perhaps because they have been so gradual, are not necessarily so noticeable although in their way, some of them individually and certainly in the aggregate, are just as fundamental.

In recent decades there has been a huge increase in the volume of legislation. Fifty years ago there were 450 pages of legislation passed by Parliament every year; now the total is seven times that amount, around 3,000 pages. In addition to that there are approximately 10,000 pages of statutory instruments every year as well as the paraphernalia, and dictats and legislation of the European Communities. Handling that increase of legislation in Parliament is not easy. A quite different change in recent decades has been a tendency to bypass Parliament, perhaps epitomised most in the beer and sandwich lunches the government had with the TUC and the CBI during an earlier Parliament. But that tendency is just as great today as it was under Harold Wilson's government. Ironically, under the present Prime Minister, there has been a substantial increase in the power and authority of the Prime Minister and her office. Other changes include the increase in the power and discipline of the parties. And of importance when considering the role of the Civil Service there has been the huge increase in the power of the executive. Whether we look at the taxation government raises, the money it spends, the employment it gives,[1] directly or indirectly – 30% of the labour force is now in state employ and coming up to 30% of the whole of our population are dependent upon the state for their primary source of income – its powers of patronage are vast. The social, economic and political implications of all this are vast also.

The basic political theory of our constitution is that Parliament controls the executive. That, after all, is the guarantee against unconstitutional government. There are two chief methods for handling the work of Parliament.

First, there are debates. A debate has its uses. Jaw-jaw is always better than war-war; that is the point of Parliament. It is a device for discussion; for reaching conclusions through discussion. But it is hardly the open-minded affair that exists when you have an academic debate about any particular subject. It is very rarely reason or oratory or argument which decides the vote at the end of the debate, for that will take place almost invariably upon party lines. Hence it is, as Quintin Hailsham wrote in his recent book *The Dilemma of Democracy*, that

"debate is more and more a ritual dance, interspersed with catcalls on strictly party lines."[2]

Listening to the BBC's *Today in Parliament* programme might suggest that that view is entirely accurate. It is not really a fair picture of what Parliament does but, like the newspapers, it is always the sensationalist thing to which we are obliged to listen or pay attention.

So much for debate. Then there is Question Time – an important constitutional feature, but if you really want to duck a difficult question it is not too hard to do so. The cynics will tell you that Question Time in the House of Commons is very largely an exercise in the issuance of non-information. There is more cross-examination of Ministers by the lobby or by other outsiders such as Sir Robin Day on the television. There is more questioning of Ministers by outsiders than there ever is on the floor of the House of Commons at Question Time.

It has been increasingly the view from inside the House that the traditional methods whereby Parliament has done its business are now inadequate. On the constitutional side, Parliament must always be conscious of its duty to sustain effective government; but increasingly control of the executive has become an obligation upon the supporters of the government of the day, not simply the duty of the opposition, important though that may be.

You can argue that each year government has to come to Parliament for money. It is open to the official opposition or to individual Members to raise the broadest issues of policy or individual personal grievances before, in the old phrase, "supply is granted". If the Government were defeated, especially on an issue of confidence, then it would have to resign and this would be followed by an election. But that is the extreme case which happens rarely. It has happened twice in recent years; once during the war and once in

1979 when Mr. Callaghan's Government was defeated and a general election followed.

But if you ask how well and how closely Parliament supervises government departments, the nationalised industries, the recipients of huge sums of taxpayers' money in the private sector, by comparison with the best commercial practices I would reply "Hardly at all." In general, we do not debate policy alternatives and examine them carefully. In general, we do not compare out-turn with forecasts. In general, policy decisions are not made on the floor of the House of Commons. The practice is that decisions are made in Cabinet, in Cabinet committees, and are then announced to the House of Commons either during debate or in the form of a ministerial Statement. Indeed, the situation reached what seemed to be the height of absurdity some years ago when two new quasi-entrepreneurial organisations were established – the British National Oil Corporation and the National Enterprise Board – and yet no machinery of any sort was produced for examining with any care what their operations would be.

In such circumstances it seemed to some in Parliament that we should look for new institutions to help do the task which the public trust us to do. I do not believe that it is the primary function of Parliament – still less of government supporters – to help the government of the day simply to pass its legislation. Parliament has a wider responsibility. In the words of Winston Churchill speaking of Kingsley Wood, the wartime Chancellor of the Exchequer, "He was a great party man. What do I mean by that? I mean he was a man who put his country's interest before his party's interest, and the interests of his friends before his own." That is no bad epitaph for a parliamentarian. So I believe that it should not be the primary function of the House of Commons, even the supporters of the government of the day, to assist government to gets its legislation passed however partisan we may be. I believe that the primary duty is to secure government accountability; to bring what the executive does under a consistent, constant and detailed surveillance; and to report on this to Parliament, and thereby to the nation. To do that effectively, two things are needed. The opportunity – and I have already said that our existing method of working does not give that opportunity – and the knowledge. After much talking, agitating, meetings, publications, speeches, all the time gathering new momentum, slowly the knowledge is gathered together.

In 1973 I was lucky enough to win the ballot for a Private Members Motion in the House of Commons along the lines of what has been argued in this chapter. After my opening speech the first Member to get up on the other side of the House was the then Chairman of the Parliamentary Labour Party, Ian Mikardo. He and I could not be more different in politics, or in outlook, but I hope we are both patriots. The view that he took was precisely the same as mine. I mention this to emphasise that this campaign for change within Parliament became an all-party matter.

Perhaps the biggest milestone in the aim to secure more accountability was when a Select Committee on Procedure was established, which reported to the House in 1978. After the general election in 1979, the newly appointed Leader of the House, Norman St. John Stevas, accepted the Procedure Committee's main recommendation that the House should establish a Departmental Select Committee system and announced to the House that he had persuaded the newly appointed Cabinet that it would be right to establish such a series of new House of Commons Select Committees. Select Committees are called such because their membership is chosen by a Committee of Selection. A dozen (later fourteen) of these Departmental Select Committees were set up, including those covering agriculture, home affairs, social services, education, science and the arts and others. Finally there was the Liaison Committee consisting of all the select committee chairmen. These Committees were given very wide terms of reference. They could look at financial matters, at internal administration, at policy, or indeed at anything they wanted; and they were given, in the traditional phrase, "the power to send for persons and papers". Not only did they have a very wide remit, but in addition they could get all the information they wanted. In a nutshell, they were given what I have said is essential, the opportunity to survey and the chance of acquiring the knowledge to help them.

These Committees were very much resented at the beginning. It was suggested that Ministers would not have the time to do the work and that their demands were unfair on the civil servants; it was said that they would take away attention from work in the Chamber of the House of Commons and so on. But they are now an accepted feature of the House of Commons scene and are well into their second Parliament. The work of the Committees involves about 150 Members of Parliament. The chairmanships of the Committees are shared between the parties. Their party membership by and large reflects the balance of parties in the House of Commons. It is for the chief opposition party to say the extent to which the minor parties are involved, but the chairmanships are shared between the Conservative and the Labour parties. They do their work in this way. First, they sit round a horseshoe-shaped table, wholly different from the confrontational nature of our work in the House of Commons itself where the two sides, government and opposition, are drawn up facing each other like roman phalanxes facing the assault of the Carthaginians. I think that these new Committees achieve a coherence and a factual approach far removed from the ordinary exigencies of the party political debate, and this gives their proceedings a character quite different from that of most of our work in the House of Commons. They are advised by a permanent staff. The total staff was 83 for all those Committees. They can also avail themselves of the services of various outside advisers engaged on an *ad hoc* basis. Those available to the Treasury Committee, of which I was Chairman in the 1979–1983 Parliament, gave, I believe, the same quality of advice as was available to the Treasury itself from people like Alan Walters, Terry Burns and so on. What were the specific results of these changes? The Committees would sit down and decide on the particular lines of an enquiry or the forms of monitoring departmental work. For example, the Treasury Committee might mount a general enquiry into the operation of monetary policy, and the work published is likely to be as good textually as anything you will find in academic books; some of the reports are more political, such as that on the effectiveness and efficiency of the Civil Service which was debated in the House again on 28 October 1983.[3] The same committee regularly looks at and reports to the House of Commons on the Autumn Statement and the Government Expenditure White Paper. History will tell us, but I think those reports help to ensure that the debate in the House of these matters is better informed, and so also the debate in the nation. The work of the Committees are critical in a constructive way. A report of the Home Affairs Committee led to the repeal of the SUS law. The Foreign and Commonwealth Affairs Committee was the first to alert public opinion to the intention of the Canadian Government, led by Mr. Trudeau, who was determined on what he was pleased to call the "patriation" of the Canadian constitution. If that advance notice had not been given by the Committee we would have had a constitutional crisis of some seriousness. These Committees looked into matters as diverse as perinatal mortality on the one hand and the operation of our nuclear policy on the other. Were the specific results impressive or not? I think they were. The fact is that there were ministers, civil servants and people from outside brought in – and especially in the case of Ministers and civil servants very often subjected to a detailed and searching examination lasting hours or days, with the committee having the opportunity constantly to return to subjects. In a word, daylight came flooding in. This accountability has had some interesting side benefits which some of us had had in mind from the beginning, but which are only beginning to be appreciated. For example, the fact that the Civil Service has been given a platform on which to speak. I do not believe that the Civil Service should be confined only to giving advice to ministers, they should be available to the House of Commons at large. To see the best civil servants coming forward and speaking in public is a great advance. Furthermore, 150 Members of Parliament were given an alternative career structure, and this is no bad thing. The whole process of accountability to Parliament, especially departmental accountability, was taken a considerable stage further at very little cost. The average cost of running these Committees is about £25,000 a year. Compared with the way in which committee work is undertaken in the United States, the contrast is remarkable. There are 55 or so major Congressional committees, hundreds of sub-committees, which have a total of some 20,000 staff, quite apart from the Offices of the Budget and the Office of Technology Assessment, all devices set up by Congress in order to counter what they thought was an unreasonable exercise of power by President Nixon.

So much for stage 1, the setting up of the Departmental Select Committees. Stage 2 is even more important. Things move very slowly in Parliament. People do not believe in making sudden changes.

Everything that I have described has an even longer history than I have indicated. But to my mind it has all been a preparation for stage 2, which may be best put this way. Years ago we had one of the best arrangements for financial accountability of any Parliament. That is no longer so. The way in which expenditure is supervised is a disgrace and is very largely more a matter of form than of substance. Those occasions when money matters are discussed are usually used as opportunities for debates of subjects of general and topical interest. Expenditures of millions, tens of millions, hundreds of millions of pounds are passed "on the nod", very often without proper examination. If you want power, you want to get your hands on the cash and control the way in which the cash is spent. If we – the people's representatives – are to have real influence and command of what is done in the name of us all by this burgeoning executive with its vastly swollen responsibilities, it is necessary for us to achieve such control. In the 1979-1983 Parliament it was agreed that three days in every session would be set aside for the debate of specific financial matters raised by these new Department Select Committees. So if these committees, besides following individual subjects of undoubted appeal will also buckle down to the careful examination of departmental expenditure, as is their duty, then this whole process of House of Commons surveillance can be taken a considerable stage further. It is not the only thing to do in stage 2; there are a whole series of others. When I was first chairman of the Public Accounts Committee, there was hardly a member of the Exchequer and Audit Department, which is responsible for auditing and reporting to the House concerning departmental appropriations, who had accountancy experience. All that has now changed, and something of the order of 10% of the 800-odd working at the National Audit Office (formerly the Exchequer and Audit Department) now do have a professional qualification. Furthermore, the process of audit went beyond the mere mathematical exercise of seeing that the petty cash in the till corresponded with the books, and the whole range of departmental activities and their relation to the question of value for money is being questioned. Apart from the work that has been done to establish the Local Authority Audit Commission, the National Audit Commission has been set up in the House to help with the work of the Public Accounts Committees and to oversee the work of the National Audit Office. A Government Chief Accountant has been appointed and the status of the accountancy profession within government has been raised, which is an excellent and important achievement. In addition I am very keen to see the whole business of departmental internal audit strengthened as was recommended by the Public Accounts Committee. In my view, the impetus for reform is there and I hope that we shall receive encouragement to introduce the best of ordinary commercial procedures and ally them to our democratic responsibilities.

We have no written constitution. The discipline for constitutional obedience is not the stated law, it is convention. Parliament is supreme. There is nothing that Parliament cannot do. It can make and unmake laws; take away liberty and even property. I do not know the extent to which the electorate think it right to rely forever upon good manners or conventions alone to regulate our national affairs through Parliament by ensuring that our constitutional niceties are maintained. I have always thought that this nation should above all set an example of democracy's effective and efficient working. There are so many old legislatures such as Canada, Australia, and also other small places which have taken their lead from us. But that really is no longer so, because we fell so far behind in our procedures. I hope that in establishing these new forms, new methods, new opportunities for investigation and these new checks, all promoting the accountability of government, including the civil service to Parliament, we are beginning to set an example to other legislatures. And I hope that all Members of Parliament remain true to their essential duty "to uphold the constitution".

Notes

1. For definitions of government employment see p3.
2. Lord Hailsham, *The Dilemma of Democracy; Diagnosis and Prescription*, Collins, 1978.
3. HC Deb Vol. 47 cols 535-588.

7

INFORMATION FOR PARLIAMENT

DERMOT ENGLEFIELD

The last two chapters have shaded in the Parliamentary perspective of the work of the Civil Service. This work centres not only on the need for Parliament to sanction many government initiatives, but more particularly on the responsibility of the civil servants' particular Minister "to inform the House", and it is for this reason that Parliament can be edgy and exacting if both Houses are not given precedence in this matter. With the growth of instant information through TV interviews or press releases and with the media men demanding immediate Government responses to crises, a Minister can be squeezed between his duty as the government spokesman in Parliament and the demands of the public who wish to know the situation immediately. Despite these pressures however, as the debate on the European Communities Bill 1972 reasserted, Parliament places a heavy responsibility on the Government to keep it informed in time of crisis, to explain its policy and to report on its administration.

Within a government department there are two organisations which concentrate specifically on helping the Minister in Parliament, namely the Private Office and the Parliamentary Branch. In many departments the latter is within the former. The Private Office, as indicated in chapter 5, gives its minister a very full range of support, from satisfying the most obvious needs to services which are difficult to anticipate. In doing this it does not differ from the type of aid given to the head of any organisation. What is distinct about helping a minister however is his public accountability – especially to Parliament. The Parliamentary Branch is even more specifically tuned into the department's parliamentary activity. Its staff are often on duty by 8 a.m. examining Parliament's business papers which will have been printed overnight and which are distributed throughout Whitehall by House of Commons staff before breakfast. They will be extracting those parliamentary questions tabled the previous day and which fall to their department, checking on the names of Members which have been added to motions, and noting amendments to bills which have been tabled. In practice then they are acting as the department's eyes and ears at Westminster. They will also be advising civil service colleagues on procedural matters, checking on any papers to be issued that day by the department, clearing with Number Ten any Ministerial statements which may have to be made in both Houses and sometimes responding to points made by officials of the House. They are in short, with the aid of their colleagues in Parliamentary Branches in other departments, ensuring that the total Whitehall response to Westminster is well organised, without overlap of effort and without failing to meet Parliament's exacting deadlines. The purpose of this organisation is to enable the government to set before Parliament its proposed policy and legislation and to report on how it is conducting its administration.

The origins of government "policy" are manifold: the pressure of party thinking sometimes expressed at Annual Party Conferences, the swift reaction to a crisis, the slow distillation of the wisdom of experts, the chance encounter by civil servant or minister with a concrete problem, these and many other reasons may lead to policy proposals. But they mostly arise at ministerial level if they are for reasons of politics or at departmental or civil service level if their context is really to improve administration. It is often not easy to distinguish between the two.

In recent years there has been a quite serious effort by government to involve those outside Whitehall in some form of consultation regarding policy. In the 1970s there was introduced a system of Green Papers (published in green covers and sometimes as Command papers) which were policy discussion documents which the government set before the electorate. In recent years however while the number of such consultative documents has increased, the manner of their publication has become more and more undisciplined. Today they may be Her Majesty's Stationery Office (HMSO) publications, they may be departmental publications and either priced or free, they may be printed or produced in a more temporary fashion and they may be for general or for restricted circulation. All those consultation documents which come before Parliament are listed in the House of Commons Weekly Information Bulletin (see appendix 4, III, L, page 165) together with the date by which comment must be sent to the department.

The next stage are the government's specific proposals, which appear as a White Paper (published by HMSO normally without coloured covers) and, "Presented to Parliament by (the Minister's title) by Command of Her Majesty". (These also are listed in the Weekly Information Bulletin.) The Queen's Government has thus made its proposals and there may be a subsequent debate in

Parliament. This can lead to minor modifications, and, very rarely to withdrawal of the proposals, but the government, backed by its majority, will normally judge itself elected to carry out its policy.

Once policy is decided upon it must frequently be translated into legislation. The first problem for the department is to get the proposed bill through the Cabinet committees and into the legislative programme of the session. Ideally, from the viewpoint of the promoters of the bill, they will get a specific commitment written into the Queen's Speech opening the session of Parliament. This speech is the occasion when the government informs Parliament not only concerning its general policy, but more specifically about its forthcoming legislative programme.

When a bill is introduced into one of the two Houses of Parliament and is ordered by either House to be printed and thus becomes publicly available for the first time, it is already very late in its cycle – say five minutes to midnight. The bill has evolved within the department, often been the subject of wide consultation with "interest groups", been worked on by the legal section of the promoting department, been through six, eight, or more printed drafts prepared by Parliamentary Counsel and has of course been looked at and approved by Cabinet committees. In communicating the text to Parliament, which promptly orders it to be printed, the Civil Service ensures that there is attached to the text of the bill an explanatory memorandum. This memorandum may start by referring to the White Paper which lies behind the bill and goes on to set out in non-technical language the bill's objective, its financial consequences together with, if possible, estimates and forecasts of any consequent changes in the non-industrial and industrial staff of government departments.

The next stage in explaining the government's legislative proposals to Parliament is the Minister's main speech to the House at the beginning of the bill's second reading. This has been carefully drafted by his civil servants to enable him to ride the tide of the opposition, and sometimes back-benchers seated behind him, who may disagree with some aspects of the bill. But the speech's political tone will be the minister's own.

A small team of supporting civil servants will have been formed to see the bill through all its stages and a number of these staff, in order to help their minister by keeping him informed, will attend throughout the proceedings whether in the Chamber or in Standing Committee. One further method of obtaining information concerning particular bills has been tried in recent years, but only on a few occasions when the bill was an uncontroversial one. The minister in charge of a bill can move that it should be committed to a Special Standing Committee which can then meet and take evidence for three mornings before Members start its detailed examination in Standing Committee. Sometimes the witnesses summoned to give evidence on these occasions have been civil servants.

Once the bill has become an Act it may be necessary to bring some of it into effect through delegated legislation. The text of the parent Act will have made this clear. These Statutory Instruments are laid before Parliament which means that they are delivered by the responsible department to the Votes and Proceedings Office in the House of Commons where they are noted for listing, first in the daily Votes and Proceedings and subsequently in the Journal, and then passed to the Library for the information of Members. In the House of Lords a similar procedure enables peers to see them in the Printed Paper Office. Debates on this delegated legislation, which are strictly confined to the text of the Instrument, may take place in the Chamber or in one of the Standing Committees on Statutory Instruments.

Policy and legislation are two important areas where the Civil Service help the government to pass information to Parliament. A third quite different responsibility is where it is statutorily necessary for a body to present an annual report and/or annual accounts to Parliament. These reports carry a different legend from the Command papers previously mentioned. They are "Presented to Parliament in pursuance of Section — of the — Act 19—". Some of these papers are ordered to be printed by the House of Commons and are published by HMSO, while others may be published independently by the reporting organisation. As with consultative documents mentioned earlier, the system of publishing is not consistent and consequently bibliographical control is unsatisfactory.

The most long standing method of Parliament collecting information is through appointing a Select Committee with "leave to report to the House its opinion and observations upon any matter referred to it for its consideration, together with the minutes of the evidence taken before it . . ."[1]. As has been mentioned in earlier chapters, since 1979 the House of Commons has had a system of such Select Committees, which are appointed "to examine the expenditure, administration and policy of the principal government departments"[2]. There are fourteen of these Select Committees covering the major departments of state and they provide the civil servants and their Ministers with a new opportunity to present information to Parliament.[3] During the 1979-1983 Parliament it was estimated that about 12,000 man days a year were spent by departments responding to these Select Committees. Some 1,327 departmental written memoranda were presented to the Committees, while 1,252 departmental officials made 1,779 appearances in order to give oral evidence. Clearly this is a formidable new responsibility for the Civil Service and it has been commented "nowhere else are Ministers and their senior civil servants questioned so closely and so publicly about their activities; or their replies evaluated so critically".[4] A great deal of this evidence, both written and oral, and certainly almost all of the evidence of civil servants, is ordered to be printed by the House and is subsequently published and sold by HMSO.

Of special relevance to the theme of this chapter and of much longer standing than these Departmental Select Committees is the Committee of Public Accounts. First appointed in 1861, it bases its work which is "the examination of the accounts showing the appropriation of the sums granted by Parliament to meet the public expenditure"[5] on reports made at the end of the financial year by the well staffed department of the Comptroller and Auditor General. The Committee is concerned with administration not policy, so it is the civil servants in the form of the responsible Accounting Officers rather than Ministers who are called to give information to the Committee, information which in turn it passes on to the House of Commons. Many civil servants have testified to the importance of this Committee, most recently Sir Douglas Wass in his Reith lectures of 1983:

"The Public accounts Committee has a formidable reputation in Whitehall, and it commands great respect from civil servants. It is well briefed and fully equipped to examine witnesses. I can assure you that few permanent secretaries who have to go before the Public Accounts Committee will allow themselves any private engagements in the immediate run-up to an appearance."[6]

Far better known than these Select Committee evidence sessions are the parliamentary questions asked of Ministers by individual Members, for answer either orally, in the Chambers at Question Time, or by a written reply. With about four hours oral Question Time in the House of Commons each sitting week, Members are able to ask ministers some six thousand oral questions in a normal length session. Questions for written answer are not restricted in number and can run to thirty-five thousand or more a session. The questions are addressed to a minister, but naturally replies are drafted by civil servants. As there is little political content in written questions and answers, they are nearly all asking for information not making a political point, in these cases the drafts of civil servants may often be the final reply. The number of these parliamentary questions, including written questions asked in the House of Lords, has nearly doubled in recent years and the brightly coloured files which the departments open for each question tabled, are a familiar sight on civil servants' desks.

Mention has been made of the growing problems connected with departmental publishing but in the case of Parliament's own papers, whether we are talking of reports of debates in the Chamber or Standing Committees or of the text of bills or House of Commons papers, there are no bibliographical problems as they are all published by HMSO. A sessional index to those bills, House of Commons papers and also to the government's command papers is prepared by the House of Commons Library and published by HMSO. A fortnightly index to Commons questions and debates is also prepared by the House of Commons Library and published by HMSO and this index forms the basis of the indexes of individual bound volumes of Hansard and ultimately of a separate index volume covering all the Hansard volumes of the session. (The House of Lords uses a different system). Finally, in connection with this library of information which the government puts before Parliament, much of it prepared by the Civil Service, there is the House of Commons Library's computer-based indexing system, POLIS, designed to help provide information on all aspects of Parliament's proceedings and papers for Members of Parliament. It is now subscribed to by over two hundred other organisations. These subscribers include not only government departments, universities and foreign parliaments but also local authorities, nationalised industries and private companies.

In recent years a new responsibility for the government to provide information for Parliament has arisen as a result of our joining the European Communities (EC). In 1972 the government accepted responsibility for informing Parliament concerning EC matters and the Civil Service are very involved in this duty. It takes several forms.

First, EC draft legislation and other consultative documents – together with the EC budget – are sent to Whitehall from Brussels and copies are then distributed by the Cabinet Office to Parliament and to the government department responsible for the subject area covered by the document. Normally within a fortnight, the government department involved delivers an explanatory memorandum to Parliament. Prepared by the Civil Service it is concerned to describe the implications of the draft legislation or consultative document and it has to be signed by a Minister. Both the House of Lords and the House of Commons have Select Committees which are required to examine these EC legislative proposals and other EC documents, together with the explanatory memoranda just mentioned. The House of Lords Committee especially, with its elaborate system of sub-committees, may well take evidence on the EC document from civil servants among others. These House of Lords reports and evidence are widely read, not least in Europe.

A second government responsibility arising from our

membership of the EC is to present a regular six-monthly report to Parliament called Developments in the European Communities, which is published as a Command paper and regularly debated on the Motion to "take note of the Report . . .". Thirdly the government lists for Members the EC meetings during the coming month and following these meetings, the ministers who have attended report to Parliament either by making a statement in both Houses, or, if they have been more routine meetings, by giving a Written Reply to an inspired Written Question. Finally, once a month, part of the Foreign Office's oral Question Time is devoted to EC matters. The means of informing Parliament on EC affairs introduced in 1973 are the traditional ones, but they do represent a considerable additional burden on civil servants and of course, ministers.

So much for the thousands of man days that the Civil Service spends drafting written evidence and notes for possible oral evidence for Select Committees, replies to parliamentary questions, legislation, ministers' Parliamentary speeches, and explanatory memoranda and policy papers etc., all reaffirming the government's need to keep Parliament informed. But there are also less publicised and less formal means.

First, members can and do write personally to ministers. The member can always be sure of getting a personal reply – though not necessarily one to his liking! Secondly, since 1836 ministers have been able to deposit papers in the Libraries of both Houses "for the information of Members". The fact that the paper has been deposited in the Library is often mentioned in Hansard, sometimes as part of a Statement or reply to an Oral question and sometimes as part of a Written reply. The system is often used when the minister does not believe the information merits publication. During the "emergency" in Kenya in the 1950s for instance, a huge document arrived which was a detailed account of the more gruesome aspects of Mau Mau ceremonies.

Finally there are the mostly informal contacts between the staff of Parliament and the Civil Service. The staff of Parliament who might be involved in this work probably number little over a hundred, while the civil servants will be many thousands. (The distinction between the two groups is very clear. Staff of the House of Commons are employed by the House of Commons Commission while civil servants are employed by the Crown.) The relationship is a delicate one as the civil servant has an overriding loyalty to his minister, while the parliamentary official has a loyalty to the individual member whom he seeks to help. Often, however, through such talks time wasting misunderstandings concerning information can be avoided and the general efficiency of government-parliament relations improved. But there is a spirit of anonymity between the two "sides" and the civil servant is always free to check the dialogue by indicating "for that information the Member should put down a question to my Minister". If the civil servant says this, then the responsibility of the Minister himself as set out in textbooks on the constitution, reasserts itself and the informal dialogue is closed.

The purpose of this short chapter has been to sketch in a little more detail the Parliamentary background of civil servants work, the subject of Part II of this book. Many civil servants may never have to give Parliament a thought but for others, especially those working close to a Minister, the institution Parliament is often at the back of their mind. Who better to indicate their viewpoint than the Head of the Home Civil Service himself. On 9 March 1973 in County Hall, Granada Television recorded Part II of their programme "The state of the Nation: Parliament"[5]. Using the form of a Select Committee, The Rt. Hon. Sir Edward du Cann, Michael Foot, John Mackintosh, Reginald Maudling and Nicholas Scott took evidence on the working of Parliament. One of their witnesses was Sir William Armstrong, then Head of the Home Civil Service. On the question of the immediate pressure exerted on the Civil Service by the House of Commons he related:

"I happened to be visiting the Welsh Office in Cardiff on the day when there had been an oil slick in the Bristol Channel. So naturally there was a great deal of activity going on and when I arrived at the office the man in charge there was beginning to get people in to start assessing the situation. The first question dealt with was – what was to be said in the House? It was not – how much mess there was on the beaches and what damage had been done . . . ? The first question was – the Minister's been on the line, there's almost certain to be a Private Notice Question . . ".[7]

And when he was asked by Michael Foot the broader question whether he thought the House of Commons keeps any control over the Executive, Sir William, reflecting on a lifetime in the Civil Service replied:

"Oh it certainly exercises some control, certainly a very great influence. Things are quite different when Parliament's not sitting. In a recess, especially the long summer recess, the feel in Whitehall is quite different – a certain slackness sets in."[8]

Whom this flatters I leave to the reader to decide.

Notes

1. *House of Commons Standing Orders relative to Public Business 1982-83*, HC 307 Standing Order 91, HMSO 1983.
2. *Ibid* Standing Order 99.
3. See Chapter 3, note 1.
4. This quotation from the review of the new Select Committee system by the Outer Circle Policy Unit appears in the First Report from the Liaison Committee: The Select Committee System 1982-83 HC 92.
5. *Ibid* Standing Order 98.
6. Sir Douglas Wass *Government and the Governed*. BBC Reith Lectures 1983, p.66. Routledge and Kegan Paul, 1984.
7. *The State of the Nation: Parliament* p.99 Granada Television Ltd., 1974.
8. *Ibid* p.98.

3

THE CIVIL SERVICE AND INDUSTRY

Chapter 8

An Overview
Dr Wyn Grant

Chapter 9

An industrialist's view – the public sector
Glyn England

Chapter 10

An industrialist's view – the private sector
Kenneth Corfield

Chapter 11

A civil servant's view
Anne Mueller CB

Chapter 12

Face to Face – a case study
Nigel East

8

AN OVERVIEW

DR WYN GRANT

In this chapter, I want to provide an overview of relationships between the Civil Service and industry as seen by an outsider. The term "outsider" is very appropriate, as like most academic experts on government-industry relations, I have direct experience neither of government nor industry. However, I do spend quite a lot of time talking to businessmen and their representatives and also to civil servants, about the problems they face in developing an effective working relationship with one another and I am able to look at these problems without the organisational commitments of a civil servant, a pressure group official or a businessman.

I want to concentrate on four general problems; these are the problems of career structure, the problems of timescale, the problems of institutions and the problems of values. There are some other particular yet nevertheless important problems which I shall ignore: for example, those faced by a firm which has a government department as a major customer, or, to put it the other way round, the problems faced by government departments in developing a satisfactory relationship with their major suppliers. However, I would argue that the four problems I have selected are of general importance in the consideration of how government and industry can work more effectively together. They are just as relevant to a consideration of the relationship of the nationalised industries with government as they are to an understanding of government's relations with private firms, although clearly there are special problems in the relationship between government and the nationalised industries which are treated in chapter 9.

Career Structure

It is now conventional reformist wisdom to regret the fact that government, industry and, for that matter, universities, have separate career structures and that the man or woman who transfers from one career to another does so at some risk in terms of their career development, not to mention their pension rights. There have, of course, been particular individuals who have successfully made the transfer, particularly from the Civil Service to industry. Increasing use is also made of secondments between the Civil Service and industry which is also discussed in chapters 3 and 11. There is no doubt that such secondments are valuable in giving civil servants and businessmen an understanding of how another important part of the world works, experience which could not be acquired in any other way. As one civil servant commented recently in a RIPA Report, "Those coming back from outward secondment assure us that they have not only acquired new skills or burnished existing ones with the stimulus of working within a different environment, but have returned to look at the Whitehall system with fresh eyes".[1] The practice of allowing civil servants to sit on company boards as non-executive directors or observers also gives those fortunate enough to take part a heightened awareness of the problems that management faces. Nevertheless, secondments still cover a relatively small proportion of the Civil Service for a relatively small proportion of their careers. Probably an even smaller proportion of businessmen take part in such schemes. There is a risk that the fresh perspective these secondees acquire outside their world as civil servants or businessmen may be quickly lost once they return to a familiar organisational environment and that any ideas they have acquired for improvements in particular in government-industry relations, may be suffocated by ingrained organisational habits and preferences. Something more radical may therefore be required: as Sir Michael Edwardes comments in his book, "If the Government is to involve itself as much as it does in industrial matters (irrespective of its political colour) then it needs the degree of interchange between Civil Service and industry which makes the French Civil Service so much more effective in this area".[2] Such an approach would not be without its costs. The loss of continuity in the Civil Service might impair its ability to function as effectively as it has done in what is after all its primary task that of providing advice and support to Ministers. As a consequence, answers to Parliamentary Questions might be prepared with less awareness of the possible range of supplementaries; compromise formulas in government documents might be less elegantly drafted. Many businessmen, on the other hand, might be suspicious of civil servant colleagues whose skills were not entrepreneurial but rather consisted of an ability to act effectively in the interface between industry and government. Such hybrid individuals might be seen as too prone to work closely with government or as wishing to seek interventionist solutions to problems that should properly be solved within the firm itself. Nevertheless, there might be some advantage in civil servants, particularly those working in the economic sphere, and some businessmen, particularly those working in large companies with close relations with government, as well as a large proportion of the staff of nationalised industries, being drawn from a new breed of men and women who saw themselves not as public servants or as business persons but as specialists in effective cooperation between government and industry. Whether it would actually be necessary to have specialist institutions to produce these individuals, or even to label them as a distinct group is open to discussions: that could well destroy the object of the exercise. What is needed is a further lowering of the career barriers between government and industry, not just to permit some individuals to cross over for a relatively brief period of experience on the 'other side', but so that the barriers are not so high that they discourage real changes of career.

Timescale

Even with greater interchange of personnel between government and industry, the problem of timescale, would still remain. The Civil Service does, of course, operate on a number of different timescales; this afternoon's Question Time in the House; this week's political crisis; this session's legislative programme; public expenditure plans for the next three years; and the lifetime of the current Parliament. In general, the timescale of business is longer. Businessmen do, of course, have to deal with immediate crises, but, as the CBI study of investment lead times in manufacturing industry shows, the majority of companies use a five-year corporate plan and in addition some prepare broader strategic projects for a period of up to ten years ahead.[3] Large investment projects take, on average, four years from development work to the start of production: many, of course, take longer. There is a clear divergence of timescale here as between civil servants and the business world, although one must be cautious about exaggerating the lack of continuity in the case of goverment policies. It is often argued that British industrial policy is characterised by considerable inconsistency, but I would argue that, in some areas, there has often been too much continuity. It is, of course, possible to point to particular sectors such as the steel industry which has suffered from sudden shifts in policy, but one should not commit the fallacy of arguing from a particular case to the general pattern of government-industry relations. The Industry Act 1972, as consolidated in the 1982 Industrial Development Act, still provides the legislative basis for British industrial policy. In the area of regional policy, it could be argued that there has been a lack of willingness to adjust policy sufficiently quickly in the face of mounting evidence that the mix of overall policy introduced in the late 1960s was not fully cost effective. Even if one takes the 1972 Act as the base date for current regional policy, the system of regional aid was in place for ten years with few changes in the way in which assistance is provided. Until that is, we had the White Paper at the end of 1983 [4]. It is therefore possible to exaggerate the problems which result from the divergent timescales of government and industry. Without entering into the controversy about proportional representation, I am not convinced by those who argue for proportional representation on the grounds that it would lead to greater continuity in industrial policy. I am not convinced that there has been general discontinuity, but even if there has been in particular cases, especially in relation to the nationalised industries, these are not sufficient grounds for tampering with the electoral system.

There is another problem of timescale which has also been mentioned on a number of occasions by businessmen. It is important not just that government takes the right action to deal with a problem, but that it takes the right action at the right time. An opportunity lost is as bad, or worse if public money is involved, as an opportunity not pursued at all. Alan Lord comments in the Royal Institute of Public Administration's collection, *Allies or Adversaries* "Decisions take too long . . . I really cannot emphasise too much that an answer is right only if it is given at the right time".[5] As Alan Lord recognises, the problems government faces in making a decision are different from those faced by business. Government has to take the effects of a decision into account over a wide range of interests, not just those of business. Many decisions require Parliamentary approval, and government has the duty of ensuring that public money is properly spent. In addition, the Civil Service may not always have as many staff as it wants to be able to respond quickly to a particular request or problem. Nevertheless, a greater recognition of the need for urgency in some cases on the part of the Civil Service may be desirable. For example, there is quite a lot of published evidence which I would endorse from my own discussions, which shows industrialists are often disillusioned by the time it takes to receive a response from government to a request for industrial assistance. Businessmen, on the other hand, perhaps need to show a greater appreciation of the constraints that public accountability places on government's ability to act quickly. This greater mutual understanding would be facilitated by changes in career structure of the kind I outlined earlier.

Institutions

However, even with more fluid career structures, much of the discussions between government and industry will take place between civil servants who have always been civil servants and businessmen who have always been businessmen. This leads to the consideration of the institutions that act as intermediaries between businessmen and government – the business interest associations – and the institutions within government and large firms which are engaged in coordinating and facilitating their relationship and hopefully promoting greater mutual understanding. I am referring to the sponsoring divisions within government departments and to the government relations divisions within firms.

One often hears complaints both from civil servants and from businessmen about the ineffectiveness of British trade associations, with one or two honourable exceptions such as the Chemical Industries Association or the Society of Motor Manufacturers and Traders. Although the comparative research is far from complete, there is no doubt that Britain suffers from a duplication of functions between associations, an overlapping of their interests and often competition between them, both for members and influence. That there has been a problem in this area has long been recognised. The CBI took an active interest in the issue in the 1960s and sponsored the report of the Devlin Commission which had a seconded civil servant as its secretary. The recommendations of the Devlin Commission did not find wide support among businessmen and interest in the subject died away. Even the present recession has generally led to rationalisation *within* associations – reductions in staff, etc. – rather than to rationalisation *between* associations. Government is reluctant to intervene in the affairs of what it sees as voluntary associations. Unlike in the case of research associations, government does not generally use trade associations as chosen instruments for the implementation of public policy. Firms have many demands placed on them but although the subscriptions to these voluntary associations are too low to be a major item in the firm's budget, the amount of a company's senior staff time taken up with association work is often considerable. However, many firms believe that they derive considerable benefits from participation in these associative activities, benefits which outweigh the demands made on senior management time. What did surprise me when I undertook research into individual company's government relations divisions was that they often have no responsibility for coordinating the firm's work in trade associations. The explanation given was that, particularly in decentralised companies, trade association work is regarded by product divisions or subsidiaries as their prerogative, with only CBI membership being a truly corporate responsibility. One consequence can be that the firm advocates different public policies in different settings without even knowing it. I understand that the head of one major company recently discovered to his horror that one product division was actually advocating a policy line in its trade association which was totally at variance with the company's corporate policy. He then instigated a review of the company's trade association work, but one cannot rely on incidents of this kind to provide the proper impetus for reform. Recent work in West Germany on business interest associations as intermediaries between government and their members shows that in West Germany, government does expect industries to be properly organised for representational purposes and encourages firms to work through their associations rather than to contact government direct, although that method may be less appropriate in a more concentrated economy such as Britain.

Values

I regard the development of government relations divisions within large firms as a positive step, despite recent comments in an Institute of Economic Affairs pamphlet that they represent a diversion from a firm's proper task of making money and that they encourage what the writer of the pamphlet chooses to regard as collusion between government and business, but what I would prefer to call cooperation. Government relations divisions can make a positive contribution to better government-industry relations in two ways. First, they can ensure that firms have a better understanding of how government works, what its policies are, and how the wider problems it faces constrain its ability to act. They can do this informally by providing an input to decision-making within the firm and more formally by providing short training courses for managers whose work brings them into contact with government. Second, they provide a mechanism for facilitating contacts between civil servants and ministers and the firm, allowing government to learn more directly how its policies are affecting firms at the sharp end, rather than hearing what is often a diluted and compromise view from a trade association.

Sponsorship divisions within government are the principal point of contact for most firms and trade associations, leaving aside special cases such as defence industry firms. As stated by government, "The basic aim of sponsorship is to help the industries to be successful, and to this end to ensure that in the formulation of policies by Government the particular interests of the industries sponsored are identified in consultation with them . . . Conversely Industry Divisions seek to ensure that their industries understand the reasons for and the implications of Government policies".[6] In short, sponsorship divisions can act as spokesmen for their industries within government, although advocacy always has to be placed within the context of overall government policy.[7] In turn they explain the policies of government to industry. They therefore have a crucial role to play in facilitating good government-industry relations. One problem has been the dispersal of sponsorship divisions across a number of government departments, although the formation of the Department of Trade and Industry has helped considerably in that respect. Nevertheless, the Department of Trade and Industry was reported to be reluctant to acquire sponsorship of pharmaceuticals from the DHSS; sponsorship of the construction industry is at the Department of the Environment; food processing at the Department of Agriculture, while many of the nationalised industries are sponsored in the Departments of Transport and of Energy. Although one must not make too much of the significance of particular organisations' arrangements, there is a risk that sponsoring divisions outside the Department of Trade and Industry may be outside both the mainstream of general industrial policy formation within government and sometimes the mainstream of policy making within their sponsoring departments. This is a particular problem as industrial policy has shifted from a vertical, sectoral emphasis, to a horizontal across the board approach, concerned with ensuring that new generic technologies are effectively developed and applied to traditional industries. The legacy of the older, vertical approach may die hard and limit the response of industries to policies of innovation when they are sponsored away from the Department of Trade and Industry. More generally, one way of improving communication between government and industry might be to give greater status and resources to sponsorship divisions, although one welcome consequence of the merger of the Departments of Trade and of Industry is that the new department's sponsoring divisions are now involved in export work in a way that they were not before.

So far I have confined my remarks to central government, but there are other forms of government which may pose greater problems in some ways for businessmen than central government. The burden placed by business rates on enterprise, particularly in some parts of the country, is a familiar theme. The efforts made by central government to cut their staff and secure greater cost-effectiveness might be compared with the lack of willingness on the part of many local authorities to make any similar effort. Some of the new jobs created by some local authorities appear likely to make no contribution to economic revival or, for that matter, to social harmony or the effective operation of our social institutions.

Although the staff of central government has been cut back, this has not been true of all quasi-governmental bodies, despite the attempts at mass quangocide a few years ago. Indeed, some of the larger bodies continue to grow and grow, not least the Manpower Services Commission (MSC). I do think that many of the things that the MSC does are very worthwhile, but there may come a time when we need to reconsider the role of this rapidly expanding organisation, sitting as it does between the Department of Employment on the one hand, and the remaining statutory training boards, the non-statutory training organisations and the area manpower boards on the other.

Another quasi-governmental body whose future must now be in some doubt is the National Economic Development Council. It is sometimes said that its main achievement has been that it has survived, and it is certainly difficult to point to many positive changes that have directly resulted from NEDDY involvement. However, its influence is necessarily of a subtle kind: it may be a talking shop, but there is some value in that, if it brings together government, employers and unions in a constructive discussion of industrial problems away from the tensions generated in the process of collective bargaining. I think that a distinction has to be made between the council itself, which is a more political body in the sense that it is sometimes used for point scoring exercises, and the economic development committees which, in practice, have considerable latitude within their steering brief, to develop their own ideas about how the performance of their sectors might be improved. I wouldn't be sorry to see the council go, but we might miss the office and the committees rather more.

One could alter career structures, bring about a convergence of timescales and even reform institutions but still be left with fundamental misunderstandings in government-industry relations because of different values held by the participants. A popular, although I think overstated explanation of British industrial decline is that it is the consequence of the persistence of a pre-industrial culture. If that is true then the conclusions to be drawn are pessimistic because cultures are hard to change, even in the long term and even if one should attempt such a project in a democratic society.

Similarly, if the values of businessmen or civil servants are an obstacle to better understanding, it may be difficult to change them, although it may be possible to achieve more and that more quickly, through the work of small, well-educated groups such as the Industry and Parliament Trust.

Of course, in a democratic society, the views of government and of business are not always going to coincide, but what is important is that each side should have an understanding of the other's perspectives, decision making mechanisms and problems. If we had different career structures, we might even be able to dispense with that word "side". If better mutual understandings could be created, then in the long run we would certainly all be better off.

Notes

1. Timothy Hornsby, *Secondments policy in the Departments of the Environment and Transport* RIPA Report, Vol 4, No 2, Autumn 1983 p.3.
2. Michael Edwardes, *Back from the Brink*, Collins 1983, p. 218.
3. Investment lead times in British Manufacturing Industry: Report of a CBI Working Party, 2 vols, 1978.
4. Regional Industrial Development, Cmnd 9111, 1983.
5. Alan Lord, 'A View from the Bridge' in *Allies or Adversaries?*, Royal Institute of Public Administration, 1981, pp43-58, p50.
6. House of Commons Industry and Trade Committee, Background Note on the Department of Industry, 1979-80. HC 367-ii, HMSO, 1980, p55.
7. See appendix 1.

9

AN INDUSTRIALIST'S VIEW – the public sector

GLYN ENGLAND

In this chapter I have chosen to make a number of straightforward points, illuminated from my own experience as Chairman of the Central Electricity Generating Board, but I have had opportunities to test the validity of these points in my more recent experience in private industry and, to some extent, in work for the World Bank and the European Commission. To a degree it is past experience specific as to time and place, and I recognise that a great deal with regard to industry-government relations is changing. While there is still often a gulf in education, training and approach which becomes apparent when industrialists and civil servants get to grips with complex issues, this does seem to me, largely under the pressure of events, to be narrowing. If industrialists read relatively recent documents on, for example, management in the Civil Service, you find many parallels with reports prepared in large industrial enterprises. In *The Provision of Management Information for Ministers* prepared in the Department of Environment in 1979 and in *Civil Service Management Development in the 1980s* produced by the Manpower and Development Office industrialists find the section headings and indeed the main thrusts on such topics as objectives, financial management and succession planning all rather familiar.

The importance of the topic "Understanding the Civil Service" [1] in the public sector of industry is self-evident. What has impressed me in looking at private enterprise main board agendas and seeing the policy items on them, is the frequency with which items of their policy have a governmental content. Currently these include enterprise zones, one of the many industrial support grants, support for innovation, energy conservation grants; or, the sort of thing I have recently been involved in, government-assisted rationalisation for the whole of an industry. Many of these subjects crop up as policy items on private enterprise board agendas. We are talking about industrial policy and therefore I am concentrating on that fairly top level in the Civil Service, a little wider than the top three grades of the Open Structure to which John Bourn referred, because I will go from Permanent Secretaries down to Principals who are the sort of people with whom one would be concerned.

To be specific about time and place, in the period 1977 to 1982 I was dealing primarily with the Department of Energy which, at that time, was recognised both inside and outside Whitehall, as not being the best of departments. In that period there were three Secretaries of State. These were Tony Benn and two financial journalists, David Howell and Nigel Lawson. All three were very competent politicians. Over that same period, there were two Permanent Secretaries. One had to put up with the problem of difficulty in communicating with his Secretary of State. The other had a caretaker role, appointed for a short period before retirement, and he had difficulty in delivering anything. None of this helped those of us anxious to make progress, and on reflection, I believe I took insufficient account of these special circumstances, a point I shall return to when offering some advice later.

I should like to start at the highest level – Permanent Secretary – and, to give some insight into their work, to introduce the minutes of a meeting that was chaired by the Permanent Secretary of the Department of Industry in 1977, Peter Cary. The meeting was called to discuss the possible merger between Rolls-Royce and GEC, where those firms were represented by their principals, Sir Kenneth Keith for Rolls-Royce and Lord Weinstock for GEC. These secret minutes were revealed in total in *The Civil Servants* .[2] My comments are quite different from those in the book.

The minutes include some directly recorded views of the industrialists who were present. The gem comes from Sir Arnold Weinstock, who said that either he ran the new company or it would never be formed. Those who know Arnold Weinstock will confirm that that sounds absolutely authentic. In contrast, those notes contain no view at all credited or debited to the civil servants who were present. It is possible that no view was expressed since the initiative for the meeting rested with the industrialists. However, the context of the note seems to indicate that the industrialists were looking for guidance. They were asking how such a proposal would be regarded by the government. But there is no record of any response by the civil servants. It is equally possible, judging from my experience, that whoever wrote the minutes, the private secretary to the Permanent Secretary, might have judged it prudent not to record some of the things that were said. I can assure you that can equally happen. The second point which worries me a little is that at such meetings very often third party industrial enterprises are talked about. In this case it was Parsons, now part of Northern Engineering Industries, which is in very much the same business, turbines and gas turbines, as the two firms represented at the discussion. The minutes record Sir Arnold's view that "there was no room for Parsons" and there is also a rather cryptic comment, again credited or debited to Sir Arnold, that "the Government might buy Parsons before it was taken over by GEC". I do not want to interpret that. The point I am making is that Parsons could well be totally unaware that their business was being discussed in that forum and would certainly not know the sort of "messages" that were being left with the Permanent Secretary in the department about the state of Parsons. For industrialists generally this demonstrates the value of being present, as, in my experience, at this level and even more so with ministers, "messages" are often much more important than closely reasoned documents. From this case study one also learns the importance of being close to the civil servants who matter to your enterprise. The final, small point is that if you look at the circulation of the note after the meetings it did not go to the industrial participants. I think that civil servants will agree that that is normal practice. If I may be didactic and draw a lesson, it does mean that if you have had a meeting with civil servants and you believe that some agreement has been reached, or that some points you have made need to be reinforced, it is very sound practice to follow up with a letter, putting down the things you believe ought to be recorded as a result of that meeting.

That is my mini case study and that is looking only at the top level, the involvement of the Permanent Secretary. I come now to the other end of my scale, that is the Principal level. Quite frequently principals are very young by the standards of industry. This is in the nature of civil service recruitment and career development. It has a lot of merit. First, it brings a freshness to the discussions. There is a wish to learn, and one can certainly contribute to their education by inviting such people to see the sharp end of operations. They are always under time pressure and it does not always come off, but the idea of such people being invited to travel to the Midlands or the North, to see an operation working, is of value to both parties. It could be used rather more frequently. That principals are rather young has the obvious disadvantage that inevitably it means they do not have much experience of the realities of the industrial world. That certainly does not inhibit a Principal expressing a view, particularly in the presence of a minister, in support of the minister's position and it is useful to be mentally prepared for this. When I took over as Chairman of the CEGB every power station construction site, along with similar projects in, for example, the chemical industry was in difficulties. It took a lot of energy and application to the special problems of each site to turn the situation round. It meant being innovative in many ways, including public exposure of the problems, by inviting the then Editor of the Sunday Times to arrange for some investigative journalism. We achieved some success and saw productivity improving at these long running sites. More importantly, based on our experience, we rethought our approach for new projects and determined new commercial and industrial relations strategies for future sites, which seem to have been well based judging by the bringing into service recently of the second stage of the Drax coal fired power station on programme and within budgeted cost. But we found ourselves in conflict with ministers in the newly elected Administration of 1979, who came to power with some rather theoretical ideas about how such sites should be managed. It was troublesome and over a period it did not help relationships between the CEGB and the civil servants when young principals energetically joined in discussions supporting theoretical concepts of their ministers having never, so it emerged subsequently, set foot on a major project site in their lives. We tried to put this right by inviting the Minister (Norman Lamont) and his aides to visit sites, including a site in France. The ministerial view remained unchanged and, regrettably, despite the evidence, so did the verbal support of the young principals. Today, two Secretaries of State, and tens of millions of pounds of abortive expenditure later, the theoretical ideas, under the pressures of the real world have first been reinterpreted and then quietly abandoned.

That story highlights one of Sir John Hoskyn's themes, namely the different way that experience is acquired in the Civil Service and in industry. In industry, individuals make progress by making things happen, and a young man or woman in industry is generally tested quite early on in circumstances where there is a high degree of personal responsibility. The point has already been made that for various reasons this tends not to happen in the Civil Service. The individual civil servant in much of his activity is in an advisory role, responsible for the quality of advice that is offered but not responsible for the actions that may follow. Some months after the Conservative Administration came to power in 1979 there was anxiety, with recollections of Prime Minister Heath's days, that the CEGB's capability of withstanding the results of prolonged industrial relations difficulties in the coal mines was not adequate. The CEGB's officers were urged at a series of meetings to increase stocks of coal and other materials, look at all the strategic materials that are essential for the generation of electricity, and buy, buy, buy. It was passed on as "It's the Minister's wish", "the message has come from Number 10". "Buy, buy" was the message. It was self-evident to those dealing with this in the CEGB that the inevitable consequence of such buying, if there were no industrial action, was that expenditure would be well above the cash limit. If there had been a strike it would have been all right, we should have stopped buying coal and other materials, checked expenditure and the balance retained. In the event there was no strike, we were significantly over our cash limit and there was a tremendous row. It certainly placed in jeopardy the reappointment of one executive director of the CEGB whose post happened to come up at that time. It is a ministerial appointment and it was at that level that the argument was going on. The question I want to raise is: where were the civil servants who were giving that advice at the time the row developed? The truth is that I do not know. It was perfectly clear that they were not in evidence and not on the scene when the row was taking place. That seems to me to be an unhappy training in personal responsibility. Clearly the CEGB was at fault. We had not followed the precept I mentioned earlier. We had not written, positively identifying the consequences of the action we were taking. That was my fault as much as anybody's; we should have. But it rancoured for sometime that those who had been pressing this policy were not on hand when it came to the crunch. Fortunately, after much argument, we were finally exonerated. The Secretary of State, in making the inevitable announcement to the House of Commons about increasing our cash limit, did say something along the lines that our overspending had all been in a good cause. However, the damage had been done not only to the CEGB, but also to the sense of personal responsibility of the individual civil servants involved.

Let me now take the Civil Service as a whole and talk about the framework within which they have operated recently. Like any other collection of human beings, they encompass a good deal of variety. In my view generalisations are not very sound and that is partly why I have chosen to use specific examples in this Chapter, not claiming that the examples are typical but simply that they have happened. If you look for guidance from Sir John Hoskyns, who does generalise, then I would suggest you read what he actually said in the lectures to the Institute of Fiscal Studies and the Institute of Directors rather than rely on a memory of press reports [3]. It is worth recalling that at the second lecture he said about the first lecture "My aim was not, as some people thought, to blame the Civil Service for Britain's decline" [4]. His most significant criticisms were of politicians and, as he was speaking of a particular time, primarily Conservative politicians. Within the Civil Service there are at any one time departments which are good and those which are not so good. As I have already mentioned I think it fair to say – and many people close to Whitehall would support my view – that at the time to which I refer dealing with some parts of the Department of Energy was problemmatic. There is plenty of evidence that in departments there is scope for the quality of leadership. The Minister, Permanent Secretary, Deputy Secretaries

– preferably all together – can alter the ethos of a given department. It can change quite quickly and one should recognise this in one's working with them. But given the variety of frameworks within which they work and the variety of personalities concerned, one gets a range of human response in exactly the way one would within any enterprise. Recently it has become clear that the expectations of promotion for many of these people have not been fulfilled and prospects are not there in the way they were when they had joined the Civil Service. Some civil servants reacted with a very strong wish to please, primarily to please the Minister. At a time when ministers did not appear to welcome news of success in public enterprises, it was sometimes difficult to persuade some civil servants to pass on a balanced view. They did not want to be the messenger carrying what the Minister might think of as bad tidings and more than once I was told "I cannot say that to the Secretary of State". There has been a range of response in the Civil Service to criticism, particularly when it has come from Ministers. And the media treatment of the Civil Service especially in connection with Sir John Hoskyns' thesis, has undoubtedly had its effect. This is partly so because much of this criticism has been very generalised, condemning those who are doing all the right things along with those who are alleged to be doing the opposite. That is something which the chairman of a nationalised industry is accustomed to, but it was a relatively new experience for civil servants. It has hurt and it has influenced the way in which some people work. Sir Edward du Cann speaking in a debate on 28 October 1983 linked low morale with what he called the attacks, overt or covert, on the Civil Service. I think one should recognise these possible pressures.

The lesson to be learnt regarding industry-government relations is that it is very important for people in industry to know their contacts as individuals, not just to know the general characteristic of civil servants but the specific characteristics of the people with whom they are dealing. One needs to know the framework, including the emotional framework, in which they are working at any time; and, picking up a point in chapter 2, one needs to know something about the approach to the job and the values that civil servants bring to their work. This is just the way you would try to make judgments about anyone you worked with who was involved in some particularly difficult piece of work.

In industry we know that key staff give of their best if the strategy is clearly defined, perhaps through a corporate planning process in which the way forward is argued about by senior staff, adopted by the board, and then is accepted by all those concerned. Until recently a civil servant has been rather fortunate if he has been working within any such well-defined strategy. Civil servants working with public enterprises have been struggling to achieve a good relationship between department and enterprise when Ministers have not known what they wanted. On what industrialists would regard as a comparatively straightforward matter, namely payment for costly Ministerial intervention in the affairs of a public enterprise, there are no clear ground rules. An example happened early in 1982, when Nigel Lawson, then Secretary of State for Energy, asked the CEGB, unwisely and unnecessarily, to divert from its commercial operation in a way that, within a few weeks, pushed our costs up by some £15 million. I told him at the time that it was like burning one pound notes in power station boilers. To the detriment of good working relationships, civil servants were then involved in an intense argument about who should bear the extra cost. The argument ended, at the Secretary of State's insistence, with an arrangement, which I regarded as immoral, which left the electricity customer meeting £5 million of that extra cost. I expect that now two years later similar arguments will be going on, but still with no agreed ground rules.

Industry is of course by no means perfect in this respect and there are many enterprises where a clear strategy and framework does not exist. But compared with industry there are still relatively few civil servants fortunate enough to be working with such a framework. I believe that this situation may be slowly changing. For instance the document *Department of Trade and Industry: Strategic Aims* (appendix 2) is a good indication of the new thinking. It is the first such document to be issued by a government department, and it is an excellent move forward. However I would reaffirm the uncertainties regarding industrial strategy for those civil servants who are working with public enterprises. On occasions a line of policy has been followed but then it has been pulled back by the action of a minister. This clearly creates great difficulties for effective working. In private enterprise, if I have read the signs correctly, there is at the moment a good deal of struggling to discover whether there is any coherence in the government's competition policy, struggling, that is, to make sense of what appear to be inconsistent decisions to refer or not to refer particular matters to the Monopolies and Mergers Commission. Again it is an area where I suspect that the civil servants concerned must have the greatest difficulty in doing their work. It is consistent with our experience in industry that in these circumstances there is a temptation for the civil servant to retreat into detail instead of dealing with the major issues which need to be faced. It is a natural reaction in some people to ask for information almost for the sake of asking for it; to play pat ball, letters going backwards and forwards, not actually advancing the cause. But you can sometimes recognise that the cause is not being advanced because the policy is not clear against which it should be advanced. These are features of what happens when there is uncertainty among civil servants. To try to improve the relationship, I believe that there is an obligation on us outside the civil service, in industry, to do all we can in our contacts to maintain clarity of purpose as to why we are there, and to be clear about our own principles concerning the nature of the requests that we are making.

I can be more specific for public enterprises where the government is exercising the shareholder function. I am sure there would be less conflict and confusion if, whenever industry and government met, those in the discussion on both sides tried to maintain with absolute clarity the basic principles that the Minister and the department are interested in the broad strategies and the way forward for the enterprise, whereas the board of the enterprise is totally responsible for running and managing the enterprise itself. These are simple propositions which are often lost sight of in the nature of the industry-government interchanges which take place. If we did this – and I am putting the obligation on the industrial side as much as on the Civil Service – then I think we would help to clarify where specific responsibility rests and make it replace second guessing, which is something that tends to happen from time to time. Industrialists should increasingly make the identification of responsibility the real issue of these meetings and if in your discussions with civil servants you find the word 'Treasury' being mentioned as an alibi and as tying the hands of a department, then simply ask that a Treasury official be present at the next meeting. This can be quite effective.

In conclusion it is an elementary point that there really is need for better mutual understanding as between industry and the Civil Service, concerning the ends and the means of both parties, particularly at times of rapid change. I can echo the point made at the end of Chapter One that, for a variety of reasons, not excluding the fact that times are hard for all of us and we are all struggling that little bit harder, there are indications that, in seeking this clarification, industry and civil service are coming closer together.

Notes

1. This was the title of the original Industry and Parliament Trust seminar on which this book is based.
2. Peter Kellner and Lord Crowther-Hunt, *The Civil Servants*, Macdonald & Co. 1980.
3. *See* chapter 2 Note 3.
4. Sir John Hoskyns, *Conservatism is not enough*. Annual lecture to the Institute of Directors, 28 September 1983.

10

AN INDUSTRIALIST'S VIEW – the private sector

SIR KENNETH CORFIELD

"In politics we have not yet found firm, reliable ground. Here there seems to be no clearly established order; we are always threatened with a sudden relapse into the old chaos. We are building high and proud edifices; but we forget to make their foundations secure."

Ernst Cassirer *The Myth of the State*.

The Civil Service has traditionally acted as an impartial adviser to government, and as the executor of government policy. Industrialists therefore interface with the Civil Service in two ways. First, by laying out facts and views on issues affecting industry when they are of national concern so that civil servants have had as wide an exposure to issues as is practicable, where they have to advise Ministers. Second, because the Civil Service implements government policy and industry operates in a market whose activities are directly and indirectly affected by government – through purchasing, R & D support, grants, regulations and so on.

The ability to do two apparently contradictory things at the same time – to advise impartially and to execute with similar impartiality – is the product of the British Whig tradition, fostered by the liberal tradition of education and seen explicitly in the liberal professions, amongst which is the Civil Service ranking with medicine, law, finance and academia. These professions are distinguished by their integrity, and an ability both to analyse objectively and to argue a case dispassionately. At the end of the day, the outcome is a product of the *humanitas* of education: a seeking of the truth, but in the knowledge that the truth cannot ultimately be judged. It leads therefore at a practical level to consensus or the application of conventions.

This is not the way of industry, which shares the need for all these qualities but which differs in its requirements by the further need for a commitment first to take the ultimate responsibility for making something and then of selling it to a customer. On this criteria industry is judged.

This distinction between the work of the Civil Service and those who are in industry is made not to question the benefits of the liberal tradition: it is simply to point out that the tradition in which the Civil Service has developed is in part alien from those in manufacturing industry. This is the foremost barrier between industry and the Civil Service and it is one which has not gone unrecognised.

In the past decade, efforts have been made both by industry and by government servants to build bridges between each other. Secondments in both directions have been introduced. Most significantly, government actually recognised the importance of industry by creating a Department of State responsible for its interests; the introduction of "sponsor divisions" [1] in the Department has brought civil servants closer to industry by their visits and contact on social occasions. This sponsorship has led to several other activities, the most significant being the introduction of state grants and other types of support. All this has necessarily meant that the civil servants concerned come to grips with how a company functions: what a balance sheet means; how cash flow works; the meaning of profit; how products are planned and launched and how R & D is organised.

At the end of the day, however, these are mere nibblings at a fundamental problem which is that while Britain's social and defence policies may depend upon its economy's capacity to create wealth, the industry which creates this wealth operates in a tradition which is essentially alien to wealth creation. Industrialists operate in a culture which they perceive to be hostile to their interests; industry's roots are not the common ones shared by the city, professions, academia and the Civil Service. The liberal tradition of education has created an ability to understand intellectually the issues and to propose solutions, but this is not the same as creating a culture imbued with an appreciation of how to make and do things and how to make industry succeed. The consequence of this fundamental problem is the parlous state of the British economy.

To understand how civil servants and industrialists work together today, it is important to understand then, the traditions and subcultures within which each group "operates" and out of which they have grown. Our understanding of industrialists' actions and perspectives cannot however be divorced from the overall performance of the British economy, and the effects this has had on the way in which successive governments have perceived this problem and developed policies to address it. The application of such government policies has underpinned Civil Service-industrialists relations, as civil servants are carrying out government's policy.

Britain's economic performance has been a major preoccupation of British governments since the middle of the nineteenth century. By the end of the nineteenth century a decline had started in the British rate of increase of industrial production relative to that of her competitors. It was widely written about and debated at the time, both in Britain and overseas. The acknowledgement of Britain's early superior performance had led to reforms of technical and engineering education in Europe and the USA in order to make their systems more vocationally orientated. Public works programmes were also initiated to stimulate national economies; scientific research was publicly funded; early sickness and pension benefits were introduced, not just in response to the social plight of the populace but in recognition too that the social consequences of industrialisation had to be mitigated so as to support the industrial machine itself. Britain's response was less sanguine. From the 1880s, secondary technical education came under scrutiny at frequent intervals by philanthropists who funded technical training institutions, and by the government which set up enquiries into the state of secondary education. But the government of necessity rather than voluntarily became drawn into recognising and acting upon the social consequences of industrialisation.

Industrialists themselves, bred in the laissez-faire tradition, did not encourage government intervention other than in limited ways. Thus, whereas overseas a fundamental response to Britain's early industrial success had been orchestrated by foreign governments (perhaps no more than was to be expected within Roman legal and jurisprudential traditions), in Britain itself government was less responsive to her plight because what had bred success before it was presumed would do so again.

This created a relationship between government and industry which has been perpetuated to this day; it is typified by industry's suspicion of "intervention" on the one hand, and a curiously paradoxical recognition that the government has a responsibility towards industry on the other. The gap is one of a failure to tackle the fundamental concepts underpinning cultural differences between government and industry and so to build up practical courses of action. In consequence, the pace of Britain's decline accelerated.

The full impact of this decline can be seen in the UK economy's more recent performance. Overall, the OECD economies grew more slowly in the period 1967 to 1978 than in 1957 to 1967, but in the same years the rate of growth of the UK economy was slower than most and reached only 60 per cent of the OECD average. Her share of world trade declined from 15.1 per cent in 1963 to 8.5 per cent in 1982. The non-oil visible trade balance moved from a surplus of £170 million to a deficit of £2,486 million over the same period. By

1983, one-third of the deficit in manufactured goods was made up of electronics products which just five years before had produced a trade surplus. In other words the manufacturing part of the economy had become unresponsive to the change in markets; Britain has not been taking sufficient share of the fastest growing world markets to help her economy to attain the aspirations of her citizens.

This economic decline of the UK has a direct impact on the social welfare of the nation. In 1965 the UK ranked above France, Italy and Japan in real gross domestic product per head and was 96 per cent of West Germany and 68 per cent of the USA. By 1977 both France and Japan had overtaken the UK and the ratio of the UK to West Germany had fallen to 81 per cent. Britain's people are, in short less well off in terms of income and services than those of her major industrial competitors.

Britain's relative economic decline then became the central preoccupation of successive administrations after the Second World War. The means of reversing the decline have become the centre of political and ideological debate, which ostensibly plays tug-of-war between government and therefore civil servants and industry. Britain's major competitors on the other hand have adopted a more pragmatic approach, building on the traditions of the policies they adopted at the end of the last century. These traditions recognised that governments have responsibilities towards their economies as they do towards other matters affecting their citizens.

The government's responsibilities began with the defence of the nation, continued through to the enforcement of law and order and have been extended to include the social well-being of the individual. It is intrinsic for government to interest itself both in the management of the economy and the nation's social policies. The interplay between the different parts of these government responsibilities is self-evident. Government expenditure on defence, law and social welfare is so great that it has a major impact on the economy; de facto government has a major influence on industrial performance. By extension it is arguable, that government has a de jure responsibility to do what it can to promote the economic performance of the nation.

The Civil Service is the pivot between government and industry, and the interplay between industry and the Civil Service is variously determined by the policies pursued towards the economy and specifically towards industry, from one government to the next. This raises two fundamental questions. First, how has industry perceived the industrial policies of successive governments? Secondly, in implementing those policies, how has industry interacted with the Civil Service both to ensure that civil servants in their advisory roles to ministers relay an accurate statement of industrial requirements, and on the other hand how has industry ensured that the best advantage accrues to industry in the implementation of government policy?

The role of government towards industry is at the centre of political debate about economic policy. The debate has been about intervention versus non-intervention. The reality is that governments of the major principal parties have become increasingly interventionist. Arguably the most interventionist industrial Act[2] ever passed in this country was that of the Conservative Government led by Edward Heath. No government since then has significantly reduced the powers conferred on the Secretaries of State concerned with industrial performance (Treasury, Trade and Industry, Employment) by that Act and its successors. It provides a major enabling mechanism for any government of any political conviction to pursue its objectives whatever they are; it provides for example reserve powers to deal with industrial situations where it is deemed to be in the national interest to "preserve" industrial capability. Government's modern role means that it cannot even tacitly condone poor economic performance and consequential social decline.

The problem for the industrialist in the United Kingdom has been the inconsistency of successive governments in their public statements on industrial policy. The situation is however paradoxical. Governments have become successively more interventionist and have adopted to all intents and purposes, the same instruments to implement their policy. However, the economic system is not built simply upon actions, but on the perceptions and beliefs of what is likely to happen. For example, the belief that a "left-wing" government will be put into power can depress the stock market; if share values fall the scope for borrowing for investment by companies is reduced and they hold back on investment plans. Perceptions thus become realities and a lowering of output results. So whilst the practices of one party have common ground with those of another, the belief that they are different can, in practice, induce a change in performance.

Industry's relationship with the Civil Service however still remains consistent because as a result of its changing policies, government forces both the Civil Service and industry to work on a pragmatic basis, problem by problem. The fundamental cultural divisions between them remain unstated and so unresolved. At the working level of sponsorship, for instance, business carries on from one year to the next as specific issues are taken up and practical solutions are reached. What is absent however, is a means by which these individual actions fit into a coherent framework which assures long-term sustained economic growth. And this is because industry plans against real business opportunities tempered with the recognition of its social and political responsibilities, while governments plan to a political ideal tempered with reality.

The debate about industrial policy has been conducted at a national level in Britain between the two major parties. The impact of a change of party in government can affect performance, but other countries too have two party systems yet they do not have similar experiences when government's change. The most apparent radical change in recent years amongst the industrialised economies has been the election of the socialist administration in France. Major change in economic management was coupled with an extensive programme of nationalisation. For the first two years, the economy was depressed, partly due to the "reforms", and partly due to the world-wide recession. Although the effects of the policies led to changes in economic management, the underlying process of adjustment in industrial infrastructure, if temporarily slowed down by the state of the economy, has continued. The French, and other industrialised nations, seem to have a greater ability to create an environment in which industrial policies are pursued more consistently. This is because at a deeper level of politics – at a cultural level – there is a greater appreciation of what industrial policy really is, and this understanding transcends mere political changes.

We cannot ignore this, namely other countries' industrial progress through policies which are fundamentally more consistent, because in Britain we trade internationally, and other governments' policies are factors which affect our international competitiveness. For example, major capital projects require large "up front" funds which involve high levels of risk. The competitive position for Britain as an exporter is made even tougher when overseas customers, especially when they are influenced by their own governments, impose conditions which heighten this risk. Long-term guarantees of performance in major projects such as submarine systems are required when only one failure in 25 years of operation is typically acceptable to customers. This involves exceptional risk to a supplier. If a UK company takes such a risk, the efficiency of the "capital" markets become counterproductive: share prices are written down because the risk is thought to be too great, and the financial sector cannot offer insurance cover except at prohibitive rates. Government could act as a lender-of-last-resort. However, the naive political attitude emerges that if the financial markets are not willing to take the risk, why should government? The attitude is "naive" because it represents a narrow understanding of the nature of competition; it is a view that the market stands alone, and is divorced from government, rather than a recognition that government is part of it. Industry's relationship with civil servants is strained in such circumstances; within what is possible and allowable, they accord every sympathy and support, but the fundamental issue remains untackled because the civil servant is the "appendage" of a continuing unrealistic political system.

The purpose of industrial policy is not to supplant the market mechanism, but to provide a vehicle to generate mutual understanding within industry and government of the changing natures of markets and technologies, so that both industry and government adopt policies which ensure the country's long-term economic and social goals. With regard to firms, the policies are meant to assist them in their planning and production; there are no general solutions to the multifarious ways in which firms respond to technological and market opportunities. With regard to government, however, planning is meant to ensure that the state's activities – direct (investment assistance, R & D funding, nationalisation and so on), intermediate (purchasing), and indirect (regulatory, macro-economic, demand and monetary management) – are coordinated and used to sustain the industrial infrastructure in the face of changing technologies and markets. And this should be done by selective action to assist firms in developing competitive advantages so they may increase their share of the world market.

In higher technology, there is increasing understanding of what business strategies are required if firms are to grow in real terms over sustained periods. For example, for some years it has been well understood that costs are reduced in high technology business by 20-30%, for each cumulative doubling in volume.

The success of overseas firms – especially Japanese ones – is clearly associated with their high shares of world markets and hence their high volumes, relative to the size of the available market. Volume has given them greater commercial strengths, with the benefit of production economies and consequential low costs, together with a large base over which to recover R & D costs. High volumes relative to the available market do not, however, in themselves explain how these firms have attained internationally competitive positions. It has occurred because these firms have distinguished between different types of cost structure and other competitive factors which characterise their various businesses internationally. Such an understanding is critical for firms in internationally traded businesses, since it is the characteristics of these businesses and how they differ amongst their international competitors, which determines the strategic options open to them, and therefore the means of increasing their share of the market.

If we look at a business such as semi-conductor wafer fabrication, the major part of the costs lie in production and design engineering. Depending upon the particular type of product, they may account for 40-50% of the costs, and it will largely be in concentrating effort to reduce costs in that part of the business that firms will achieve competitive advantage in international markets. In this case, the development of more sophisticated Computer Aided Design systems will be critical, as will advances in material sciences. In both these areas, technological advances are likely to bring competitive advantages in wafer fabrication, and shift the key competitive factors elsewhere. This may not always be the case.

In 1979, the National Economic Development Office carried out an international comparative cost study of the colour TV industry. It was found that the single chassis design of the Japanese brought direct competitive advantages: not only were there less components than in a British TV set which was multi-board, and therefore less opportunity for things to go wrong, but the simplicity of the Japanese design meant that automated insertion techniques could be used in assembly. Simplicity of design and subsequent ease of manufacture meant that reliability and quality were substantially enhanced, while costs became highly competitive. There were, of course, other factors at work, but it was primarily in the design and manufacturing process that the major costs lay, and it was on improving these that the Japanese concentrated. In response, the appreciation of a comparative international cost study led to a concerted policy by both the government and companies to restructure the UK industry. It has been relatively successful but it came too late really to redress the balance of advantage held by the Japanese and their satellites. Such developments did not therefore depend on major technological advances (the technology was substantially bought in), but on simplicity in its use.

Alvey [3] also came too late to address the wafer production issue; the problems only become identified "politically" that is, by government, when they are visible because of a loss of competition. The Civil Service – and its political masters – needed earlier common rigid business analysis, in order for us to be internationally competitive. It is such rigid business analysis, shared between industry and the government, that determines where and how the major industrial nations are placing their resources. And the objective is to use our national resources to build the international competitive edge of businesses. In this way, the efficiency and benefits of the allocation of resources through the market are not in conflict with, but rather can be reconciled with, social objectives. Social policies and economic policies must be mutually supportive. This means industrial policy is in part at least, concerned with solutions reconciling economic and social objectives.

An example will help illustrate the principles involved. In simple financial terms the public sector is dominant in the electronics industry. It consumes one-third of the output of the industry and in some sectors as much as 80 per cent. Over half the national R & D expenditure on electronics comes from the government. And through investment assistance and the like, as much as 5 per cent of the gross investment of the industry comes from the government. It also trains and educates the industry's human resources. In other words the public sector is the single most powerful influence on the electronics industry and one justification for an industrial policy is that optimal advantage can be taken of the activities of the government. The UK's major international competitors do precisely this in recognising that the government, as part of the market, has a continuing transparent role to play in the development of any industrial society. Although the ways in which foreign government's operate differ, they share both continuity of policy to assure the strengthening of the industrial infrastructure, and continuous dialogue with industry so that their actions reflect and reinforce industrial developments. The UK's competitors official policies directly help improve the international competitiveness of these firms, and in this way help raise the efficiency of their industries in international competitive terms and hence the living standards of their people.

Government industrial policies are, in reality, becoming a major feature of international trade. Failure to recognise this hampers those economies whose public sector activities are not directed towards improvements in competitiveness.

The underlying reason for the failure to develop industrial policy in Britain lies in the failure to develop a technological or industrial-based culture. The common feature of our major successful industrial competitors is that at the level of leadership in their societies, not only are mechanisms in place which generate an appreciation of industrial priorities, but the quality of leadership has been fostered through the education system. A mobile elite supported by a broadly based and technologically orientated education system assures links across different socio-economic groups. The ultimate strength of the Japanese, the German and the French does not lie in their technology, skills or quality of investment, nor any single identifiable matter, but in their possession of an education system and set of attitudes which do not make invidious distinctions between different parts of society.

Dialogue between industry and the Civil Service is currently taking place in the context of a declining economy and a dominant public sector. In terms of interpreting specific industrial issues and advising Ministers on policy, the British Civil Service is exceptionally qualified. It is a product of an education system structured to provide dispassionate analysis and impartial advice, and to carry out ministerial wishes; these qualities are the hallmark of the liberal professions amongst which the Civil Service is one.

Industrial production developed in Britain when the feudal structure was still very strong and industry-derived wealth overlapped and was contemporary with an aristocratic society. The newly-affluent adopted the life style of a leisured aristocracy. The underlying philosophy of British education was class based and rooted in the liberal tradition. The grammar and public schools and the university system influencing the values and content of their curricula were almost exclusively middle class and pursued liberal and humanitarian studies, with little or no vocational scientific or "practical" context. The artisan was the cornerstone of technical education, and whilst the need for the industrial worker, the mechanic or artisan to have a knowledge of science was recognised, it was only linked to industrial practice. At all levels technical and engineering education in Britain was unfunded and unled. This stratification and the failure to develop a mobile managerial elite, aware of how wealth is created, means there is interpretation without understanding.

Change cannot be effected overnight: it will occur as existing relationships and controls are developed, but it will only ultimately be brought about, when, as her competitors did in the nineteenth century, Britain through her government tackles the fundamental issues of education and training to create a society in which it is appreciated that wealth creation is not alien to other social and cultural developments, but rather that it is fundamental to them. This alone will develop an environment in which there is no more than a small gulf between industry and the Civil Service. It is not a question of intervention or non-intervention, but one of reconciling through mutual appreciation the role of the government with the role of the market. It is a pragmatic issue and not one of ideological dogma creating intellectual and cultural business.

Notes

1. *See* appendix 1.
2. Industry Act 1972 cap. 63.
3. *See* appendix 3.

11

A CIVIL SERVANT'S VIEW

ANNE MUELLER CB[1]

I should like to start by describing in a general way the functions of government in relation to industry, then by looking at some of the differences between government and industry which affect their relationship, and conclude by looking at ways of improving this relationship, including the understanding of industry within government, and hopefully the reverse as well.

The functions of government in relation to industry are very pervasive and affect the whole of Whitehall in one way or another. In the first place setting the climate for industry is an essential function of government wherever it may be. That embraces the macroeconomic framework in which industry has to operate but it also embraces the legal framework, including commercial law and international treaties, because these are very important for the flourishing of the trading sector in addition of course to the framework of law and order.

Secondly there is government's function in terms of national housekeeping. Government has to raise revenue to pay for its own costs and this taxation in one form or another affects every business and at different levels. Although their primary function is to raise revenue, we have seen, since the war, taxes being developed with explicitly economic objectives in view. For example investment incentives in the form of special arrangements for writing off capital expenditure which has been with us since the late 1940s. (*Note* the 1984 Budget introduced important changes to these.) The other side of this national housekeeping is the government's public purchasing function. Every department of government buys goods and services on the market. The most important by far is the Ministry of Defence with its massive defence budget. That department is inevitably very close to industry in the exercise of its purchasing power and in its sponsorship of research and development needed for defence.

Thirdly there is the regulatory function of government, regulation which is seen by government as necessary to protect consumers, workers, investors, even inventors, and to protect local residents – a basic responsibility of government in all societies, which again has important impacts on the business sector. More recently, we have also had regulation to promote efficiency, including the efficiency of the business sector. I mention competition policy and restrictive trade practices legislation just as an example.

I shall not say much about another aspect of government's relationship with industry namely its sponsorship function as this is described in appendix 1. It is interesting that historically the sponsorship function started in wartime – in the first world war and was then reintroduced in the second world war when it was referred to as a production function. The objective was to administer scarce materials in wartime in order to meet national priorities. It has been continued and developed in peacetime as a broader, sponsorship responsibility on the lines described in appendix 1. I do not regard such sponsorship as lobbying for particular industries within government; there maybe an element of that but departments need to be critical lobbyists because, at the end of the day, government is interested in total economic performance and a department just acting as a protectionist lobby is unlikely to be contributing to improved performance. It has been suggested in chapter 8 that it may be a weakness that the sponsorship function is scattered round Whitehall rather than being concentrated in the Department of Trade and Industry. I am not so sure about that; of course you can always debate the best way of putting together the functions of government. My own view is that the pharmaceuticals industry is so dependent on the National Health Service in this country as its major market, that there really is a benefit in having sponsorship of the industry and its major client by the same Secretary of State. But there may be a case for closer coordination of the various sponsoring functions with Whitehall; I would not debate that. The Department of Trade and Industry, and the Department of Industry before it, has always regarded itself as having a responsibility in relation to the nation's business sector as a whole, not just confined to those industries which it sponsored. Finally, I ought to mention the government's role as shareholder. A large part of the business sector has been nationalised since the war, very important elements in the total economy have been set up as statutory corporations, and the control of that sector has been an important government function in the last 30 years. This aspect is treated in greater detail in chapter 9. I should also mention concerns incorporated under the Companies Act which are owned by the government in whole or in part. Two large ones have been taken into public ownership during the last decade or so – Rolls-Royce and British Leyland, though there has always been a hope that they might be returned to the private sector.

I should now like to focus in particular on the Department of

Trade and Industry. It is the department which is closest to the business sector, certainly in terms of sponsorship and some of the general policies which are related to that role. A short guide to the Department of Trade and Industry as it is constituted today is set out in appendix 3, showing the department's functions, and who does what at senior level. It is updated every six months or so, and is automatically distributed with the department's journal *British business*. The organisation of the department consists of what one might call vertical divisions, which are the sponsorship divisions covering particular sectors; there are also horizontal divisions, such as the general policy division which has central co-ordinating functions, the small firms division which covers the small firms sector right across the economy, the research and technology divisions and so on. Finally there are other functional divisions, for example, competition policy, consumer affairs, company legislation, regional policy and others.

There is also a publication which sets out the Department of Trade and Industry's strategic aims. This is set out in appendix 2 and is probably the first time that a department has sought publicly to state its aims. Presentations have been made to the CBI and various groups of industrialists and the reception has been very positive. People have very much welcomed it, which is encouraging and suggests that it should be updated. The plan of our strategic aims (see page 129) talks about the climate for industry. In order to improve the climate for industry the Department of Trade and Industry must rely heavily on other departments; particularly the Treasury and the Revenue departments in relation to the macroeconomic climate and fiscal policy. But there are many other departments. For instance if one is talking about human resources for industry one turns to the Department of Employment, the Manpower Services Commission and the Department of Education and Science. It is an important part of the department's job to relate to such departments in order to try and influence them and their policies so as to meet the needs for a more efficient, effective and successful industry as we see it. I think that we have achieved quite a lot in this business of influencing other departments' policies over the last 20 years or so. There has been considerable success. Since the 1960s a new relationship has developed with the Treasury, partly due to the influence of Sir Douglas Wass. Among other things he reorganised the Treasury to make sure that there was a section which was concerned with industrial policy and matters which would help to ensure that the macroeconomic climate was more conducive to a successful industrial sector. Similarly progress has been made in relations with other departments. For instance the introduction of tax relief for risk investment in enterprises needing new capital. First called the Business Start Up Scheme it was substantially widened in 1983 and renamed the Business Expansion Scheme. We were very keen to see a tax incentive of this kind to complement the long established incentives to invest in personal pensions, life insurance and house property. Altogether a lot of progress has been made since the 1960s in improving the climate for industry.

What are the differences between the work of government and that of industry? Wyn Grant in chapter 8 has already touched on some of these, particularly the differences of timescales and constraints, and of course the essential differences in function. The government's regulatory responsibility does not have an equivalent in industry; on the other hand, the government has no experience of operating in markets. I am not speaking of purely financial markets where of course the authorities are directly involved. The industries that government owns tend to be monopolies of one kind or another. Civil servants are trained to do investment appraisal and similar tasks, and sometimes this relates to projects with very long lead times such as the major infrastructure projects in the public sector. But there is no true simulation in government itself of operating in the market – the competitive situation, the importance of price and reacting to price, and the other factors which influence competitiveness. That is something that can be experienced only by direct contact with industry and, if possible, within it.

Other contributors have talked about some of the other problems which distinguish government and industry, the complexity for instance of government decision taking. There are few subjects which are not of interest to some part of government because its responsibilities are so wide ranging. There is also a need to have methods of consultation within government which reflect the collective responsibility of the Cabinet, and which consider all points of view and then produce conclusions which are often reached through compromises.

I should perhaps make it clear that legally, civil servants do not exist in their own right at all, with some exceptions such as in relation to personal accountability for public funds and recruitment to the Civil Service. Civil servants are essentially the appendages of ministers, to whom they are accountable. This is essential to the understanding of the issue of secrecy and openness. To understand that fact also helps in the appreciation of the role of strong ministers and weak ministers. If you are his appendage anyway, you obviously welcome a clear lead; no operation of government is likely to be fully effective if there is no clear direction in which you are moving, if you are simply continuing to run on a status quo basis.

My conclusion is that for various reasons the relationship between government and industry is essentially asymmetric and must always be so, but it may be that it is becoming rather less so than it used to be. There are winds of change blowing at present in the Civil Service. They have been commented on by Peter Le Cheminant in chapter 3. As he points out, the function of managing resources in the Civil Service more effectively is being encouraged, maybe rather late in the day, but certainly quite intensively. The ethos is changing. When I entered, policy formation was the interesting function in the Civil Service, the area of work which attracted the "alpha" minds. Today, there is much more emphasis on effective resource management and various initiatives have been taken by the present Government, including the greater delegation of responsibilities. Individuals working in departments are being made more personally accountable for the resources they control. For example, in chapter 1 John Bourn discussed the reduction in the size of the Civil Service. This is a form of targetry. Each department is given a manpower ceiling. My department, which was the Department of Industry before merging with Trade, has had one of the largest reductions in Whitehall – a 23% cut in staff across the board in five years since 1979. How is this achieved? They decided to give my fellow deputy secretaries and myself each a manpower budget. This is your ceiling they said, you make sure that your organisation keeps under that. There is nothing like being given a clear responsibility of that kind for making you look very seriously at the operation of the part of the department for which you are responsible, because at the end of the day you must produce the required result. It is your responsibility and this really does lead to a transformation.

Only three years ago I was given a budget for the travel and subsistence expenditure of my staff. It was £400,000, which is a not insignificant amount. Having such a ceiling is revolutionary in its way, civil servants have never had decentralised budgets in departments such as mine. The relevant rules for civil service travel, etc., are very carefully written down in a great book laying down in what circumstances you can claim travel and subsistence expenditure. The rules are laid down at the centre and all departments obey them. Provided that you meet those criteria the expenditure may be claimed. The new system created much upset at the beginning, particularly at junior levels, as people were afraid they would be prevented from completing necessary work, but today it has become accepted and it does encourage individual staff to secure better value for money spent. This is just a very modest example but it illustrates the direction in which the Civil Service is now moving.

I am responsible for the Department of Trade and Industry's regional offices. From 1984 they are individual cost centres and have to keep within their total budgets. They have a little room for manoeuvre with regard to the actual staff they employ in those cost centres, and this is a new responsibility. It is very much welcomed by the senior managers who have to operate the system. These changes which are being introduced are gradually bringing us closer to industry in our method of working and hence our experience.

There are other changes which are bringing government closer to industry and changing the nature of that asymmetrical relationship. Our accountability to Parliament is discussed by Sir Edward du Cann in chapter 6. While Parliament's supremacy is a fact, it is now subject to constraints which did not exist before our membership of the European Communities (EC). We have to observe the Treaty of Rome in this country and the EC subordinate legislation. Finally, as industry's own operations have become more complex and more international over the years, industry has become more involved in a political game, not simply a commercial game. Operations overseas immediately bring industry up against political realities and constraints and the need therefore to share experience with government.

Traditionally in this country relations between industry and government have been at arm's length. This is because historically the main emphasis has been on the government's regulatory function. That is now changing. Traditionally too relationships between industry and government have been very much at the top, with a heavy reliance on industry's representative organisations such as the CBI, trade associations and so on. What I now detect is that, as compared with the 1960s, the era of the National Plan which was imposed from the top, and where sectoral implications were carefully worked out with the help of the trade associations, in the 1970s there has been a greater realisation that government must also have contact with individual companies, to complement its relations with industry's collective representative bodies. That principle is now generally accepted and quite a lot of progress has been made.

There remain problems, of course. It is quite easy to make contact with the large companies. There are much bigger problems when one wishes to reach out to the medium, and even more so, the small company sector; but they are problems which we have to try to address.

While talking about channels of communications, let me mention one thing which helps in relation to contact with companies namely hospitality, meals and receptions. When Kingman Brewster came here as American ambassador a few years ago he made a speech in which he suggested that British management spent far too much time at working lunches and dinners. There was rather a row following that speech and I have asked myself quite often whether the time we spend at lunches and dinners is justified, especially as everybody knows that there is no such thing as a free lunch. However, my experience is that there is no doubt that you learn a great deal more about the facts of business, the constraints, opportunities, attitudes and values, across a table which is essentially a social occasion, than if you confine yourself to formal meetings. This method of contact is important as a supplement to the more formal means of communication.

Improving Communication

I should like to turn now to some of the developments we have seen in recent years which aim at improving communication and understanding between the Civil Service and industry. Historically there has been a heavy reliance, which still exists today, on advisory bodies, such as our Industrial Development Advisory Board and our Research Requirement Boards. But there are also QUANGOS with executive responsibilities, for example, the British Technology Group, the British Tourist Authority and the English Tourist Board. Having businessmen on the boards of these QUANGOS enables business skills to be brought to bear in spending the Department of Trade and Industry's funds in the most cost effective way.

Regarding the career Civil Service and the extent to which it is changing, I should like to reaffirm in the context of government-industry relations the value of "mature" recruitment. There has been in the past a practice of recruiting people over the age of 28, mainly at Principal level. These are people who have already had experience in the private sector of industry or elsewhere. It has been a valuable source of supply of people who have had broader experience and who have not come into the Civil Service straight from school or university. I should also like to refer again to joint civil service/industry training arrangements which are mentioned in chapter 4 particularly the *Top Management Programme*. Civil servants go to the business schools occasionally; they attend seminars which are attended by industrialists as well; and participate in in-house training courses run by large companies principally of course for their own staff. All this is a valuable form of contact at the individual level.

In 1968 an industrial interchange scheme was introduced for the government service as a whole, to encourage both secondments out into industry and vice versa. In 1984 there was a total of 186 secondments out of the Civil Service. Most of those were at Principal level, some higher and some lower. There were 116 secondments into the government service. The Ministry of Defence had 56, the largest number of secondments out, perhaps understandably given the importance of its purchasing function. However, it had only 14 secondments in. The other department with a large number was the Department of Trade and Industry, where in 1984 there were 41 secondments out and 39 in, so this was more balanced. Secondments generally last from three months to three years.

It would be difficult to exercise some of our functions effectively without these secondments into the Civil Service. They play an invaluable role. The Industrial Development Unit (IDU), a very professional unit set up 10 years ago, does have civil servants in it but it is chiefly staffed by secondees. The sources of its staff include merchant and clearing banks, accountancy firms, and industrial companies and the period of attachment is usually two years. These people have performed a valuable task, and there has been training and spin-off for civil servants through their participation in the work of the IDU, the unit within government which is responsible for appraising projects and applications for financial assistance and which advises the department.

We have recently set up the Alvey directorate in the Department of Trade and Industry with the remit of managing a major programme of collaborative research between the government, universities and industrial companies on advanced information technology. I do not know how we could run the directorate effectively without the secondees from firms since these people bring the essential knowledge for the department to administer this ambitious and important programme.

We have had industrial advisers for many years, ever since the Labour government of 1964. There have also been regional industrial advisers for the last 10 years. Some of these have been secondees from industry, others have been on short term contract. Our chief engineer and scientist in the Department of Trade and Industry today came to us straight from BP; his predecessor came straight from ICI. It would be nice to see more, but already we do have quite a lot of people from outside. Recently a small number of specialist advisers have been appointed to help the department's ministers. During the present Conservative administration there has been Lord Young and more recently Sir Jeffery Sterling. They bring specific skills and business experience that civil servants are not expected to have. There is also a recent scheme of short-term attachments of the kind which the Industry and Parliament Trust organises for MPs. Recently some of the companies which participate in the Trust's work have got together to try a pilot scheme of such short-term attachments to industry for civil servants.

In Chapter 8 Wyn Grant referred to the system of civil servants being appointed to non-executive directorships. This is not as formal as the industrial interchange scheme and has been operating only since 1978. It results from contacts at senior level between civil servants in the department and people in companies. To date there has been a total of 29 people involved in this scheme with specific companies. Some are observers, and some are full, non-executive directors. It provides valuable experience in dealing with real operational problems such as marketing questions which could not be simulated within government and we are hoping to expand it. Some other departments are doing the same thing, but I think that the Department of Trade and Industry is probably in the lead in this area. The individual civil servants are not allowed to accept fees. We have to try to avoid any conflict of interests or risk of impropriety, so jobs have to be carefully chosen and the ground rules clear. Subject to these a civil servant's commitment when working for a company is to that company. This is an interesting development because full secondments of civil servants are difficult to organise. They take time and each one has to be tailormade. It needs to be set up in such a way that the individual can make a real contribution to the work of the company or the department. Therefore it is an expensive process. The non-executive director system on the other hand is cheaper because less time is involved and yet there is still useful interaction. The Department of Trade and Industry will continue to give encouragement to this kind of interchange, but there are constraints. One that I have mentioned already is the reduction in manpower, which means that it becomes more difficult to release our best people. It is the best people that we try to send out on secondment because we regard it as an investment for the future. We do not send people whom we feel we can most readily spare; after all they would not be very good ambassadors anyway.

Important changes are in progress. The issue is what rate of change is manageable with our resources and within the constraints to which we are subjected, whilst at the same time preserving the best of the traditional system and the traditional virtues of the civil service, which were referred in chapter 2.

Note

1. Anne Mueller was promoted to Second Permanent Secretary in the Cabinet Office in the autumn of 1984, in charge of the Management and Personnel Office.

12

FACE TO FACE – a case study

NIGEL EAST

The most advanced plastic thermoforming machine currently available anywhere in the world is produced at the Huntingdon firm of Shelley Thermoformers International Ltd. It is good because it is microcomputer controlled, and it is microcomputer controlled because the company was able to obtain government support in 1980 for an ambitious micro-electronic development project.

An account of how industry was helped by government in a particular instance is inevitably an account of the interaction between two people. In charge of the project for Shelley Thermoformers was Technical Director Leslie Perryman: Project Officer for the DTI was Trevor Holley. Their "tales" may lack a Chaucerian dimension, but their value here is that they are very typical.

Shelley Thermoformers' story

Plastic thermoforming changes a flat sheet of plastic into a complex three-dimensional shape like the inside of a refrigerator. That the walls are of even thickness and the corners and shelf supports are as strong as they need to be is not a matter of luck. The flat sheet is heated before forming in zones (a large thermoformer will have several hundred heating elements that can each be set individually), and the process is then controlled very exactly.

Leslie Perryman joined Shelley Thermoformers in 1966 as Chief Electrical Designer to update the electrical systems which had until then been designed by pneumatics specialists. He had served his apprenticeship at British Insulated Calender's Cables and worked subsequently as a systems engineer, on the Central Electricity Generating Board's nuclear power station, Dungeness A, and on British Rail's Eastern Region electrification programme.

Within two years of moving to Huntingdon he was Chief Designer, responsible for revamping the product range and consolidating the company in the industrial thermoforming field rather than, as before, in packaging. Then came two years as Marketing and Development Director with the brief to go out and listen to customers demands – and then implement the necessary developments.

By the late 1970s, Shelley Thermoformers was a good firm – if not an exciting one – and its strengths were recognised by Andrew Deacon who bought the company to form part of a Group that could offer more of a turn-key facility. Deacon was particularly keen to push the Huntingdon firm into the export market and a Marketing Director was appointed – taking some of the load off Perryman's shoulders and allowing him to concentrate on accelerating product development.

At this time Shelley Thermoformers had a potential problem with its product range. It had the "meanest machine" on the market that could mould a refrigerator body, say, in 75 seconds using less material than any of the competitors. Some of the competitors, however, adopted a carousel approach to production rather than the conventional in-line arrangement and this brought their production time down to 60 seconds, although it was far more wasteful on plastic. Shelley had hoped that its approach would win the day but to many, it seemed, time was more important than materials.

Shelley Thermoformers could, of course, have developed the carousel approach alongside its in-line machinery, but the company neither wanted to be seen as being imitative, nor did it wish to invest in a technique that cannot handle the very cheap polypropylene sheet which loses all of its material strength at the forming temperature. The company wanted to lead the market, and automated control was an obvious solution.

"We were very tentative about it in the beginning", recalls Perryman. "We had the seeds of an idea that we ought to be in computer control, and we recognised that we needed to find someone with a good track record of converting ideas into commercial practice. But – like all the best ideas – the decision to follow this path was based on instinct rather than careful analysis: the analysis, of course, can come later. I was sitting here at my desk one afternoon, picked up the telephone, and everything grew from that."

That telephone call was to an acquaintance of Perryman – Trevor Holley of the DTI. Holley had visited Shelley Thermoformers several years previously as part of a familiarisation programme with the plastics machinery industry, and from subsequent contacts Perryman knew that the government had some schemes to aid the application of new technologies. In fact, the scheme that at that time was relevant – MAP (Microelectronics Applications Programme) was not in Holley's bailliewick, but he was able to refer the company to it, and to the preliminary phase of government supported consultancy.

Shelley Thermoformers had never before sought government support. Even when the company moved from north London in the 1960s, it looked only for local government assistance in locating in Huntingdon rather than going to the assisted development areas of the country. Leslie Perryman admits that he did have fears about red tape – a suggestion some years earlier to obtain DTI support had foundered on this problem. But the consultancy scheme arrangements were straightforward.

"We were sent a list of approved consultants and, for no better reason than they were near us, we spoke to a short-list of three. The closest of them all – Modus Systems of Letchworth – looked to have the experience we were seeking. We visited a bacon plant that they had helped to automate, were impressed by that, and their Managing Director, Nigel Smith, outlined clearly the role of consultant and client. We refined our early notions into a provisional specification, filled in some simple forms, and in three months we were well down the road and very clear about what we wanted in the way of a product, and in the way of support."

Shelley was looking to do two things with its microelectronics application. A sequence controller for the three main groups of machines was felt to be relatively straightforward, while a sophisticated heater controller was a more ambitious proposition – though one with the potential of leading to a significant reduction in cycle times with yet more savings on materials.

Government support was applied for in December 1980, and a meeting was arranged at the factory with the Executive division of MAP (Electronics Applications Division) represented by Trevor Gilpin. Although he knows his microelectronics, Gilpin was unfamiliar with the plastics machinery industry and so he brought Trevor Holley to the meeting: Holley subsequently took over as the DTI's Project Officer.

To qualify for support, Shelley Thermoformers had to show that the development was innovative and not merely reflecting developments elsewhere: this was evident from a knowledge of competitors' machines. It had to prove that the development would not have gone ahead in that form or in that timescale without support. And it had to show that the company was competent financially and managerially to undertake the task. In the event, the DTI's accountants argued at first that it could afford the development without support, but rescinded when the problems that a non-microelectronics based organisation would have were emphasised.

Leslie Perryman is cool about this phase of negotiations: they were "not ideal", he says. "You have to adopt a different style to justify the development to the DTI than for people within your own organisation. This additional justification is a strain at a time when you have plenty of worries already. But we were very pleased when we got a qualified approval on 23 February – and when they pointed out that the £91,000 we were budgeting for should be increased to £138,000 for grant purposes to allow for a development system to be purchased."

"Subsequently the documentation requested by the Department was pretty straightforward. We had to provide a quarterly report, but that was only a summary of our monthly internal reports. You do have to get your claim for the grant audited – a hidden expense that we found slightly unfair as we had not allowed for it. But generally the Department was very co-operative. Trevor was always available at the end of the telephone, and we were able to talk to him quite informally about the presentation of information. His support was invaluable as we found that we had bitten off more than we could chew: there were problems that meant that we had to extend the development programme and so extend the support period. More telephone calls and forms of course – but no real problem." The problems that were encountered were largely to do with the programming or software of the heater control application. The hardware was straightforward – some noise in the circuits being the main difficulty, but several software approaches for the heater controller had been suggested in the feasibility study, yet the one that looked most promising had to be aborted and the work begun again. Even so, the year's anticipated development programme was only marginally extended – albeit with Shelley Thermoformers and Modus Systems working through the night in the later stages to get a prototype ready for a trade exhibition.

The company's MAP application has given Shelley Thermoformers a sequence controller that precisely times the passage of a sheet through the thermoformer. It sees that the vacuum cups are "on" for the sheet feed, keeps the heater loaded, passes the heated sheet to the pressure or vacuum die, retracts the die, cools the mould, removes it . . . and generally supervises the dozens of mundane yet vital tasks that are essential to the process. Its timing is far more accurate than its hard-wired counterpart, it offers self-diagnosis of any faults that occur, and the details of the sequence can be recorded on magnetic tape to simplify setting up a repeat run.

The heater-control is part and parcel of this system, making a significant contribution to cutting changeover times for a repeat order from, perhaps, 12 hours to just one. But the responsive microcomputer system allows a further major advantage over conventional heating controls – a "Super Heat" facility that brings cycle times for the product quoted earlier down to 45 seconds, 15 seconds better than the fastest opposition.

Leslie Perryman claims that the new machine takes most of the black-art out of thermoforming. It has reduced scrap, and given greater throughput. "One has been installed in Sweden – replacing the machine of one of our main competitors. It works largely unattended and in six months the company have not had to adjust a single control. The user is absolutely delighted. The only thermoforming machines to have been exported in the last difficult years for the industry have been ours. And – with business picking up generally – there is a lot of overseas interest at the present. The Italians usually buy their machine tools at home – but they are extremely interested. They say they have never seen anything like it. We have been invited back to the USA with a very positive and exciting lead. We are working a lot of overtime here and our workforce, at 56, is our highest ever."

Shelley Thermoformers is not complacent about its technological lead – and is working now on a "second generation system". Will the company turn to the DTI for help again? "For something relatively inexpensive, like improving a system, I don't think we would. It really would not be worth the extra time and trouble. But for something more elaborate we may well try again. If more money were available – 50 per cent say rather than the 25 per cent that we received – it would accelerate industry. You need a real commitment to get a real benefit. But we are very grateful for the help we have received. Technology has been transferred to the company so that we can now employ our own designer with the confidence that we know what he is doing and why. We won't have the wool pulled over our eyes."

"I feel that Government has a vital role to play in encouraging companies to take the first steps in an unfamiliar area – whether it is adopting a new technology or exporting to a new country. The image of the Civil Service that you get from the newspapers is, of course, quite false. By and large the people we deal with are helpful and understanding, and they know what they are talking about.

"But in this field, no-one has all the answers. We don't have them, and neither does the DTI. They think that a development system should last three years, for example, whereas we know we will ruin it in one. We know that the computer is not yet robust enough to take the rigours of the factory floor without modification. But by getting together with DTI, we have got a world beating machine, we have got the experience of the technology in-house, and we have got confidence."

The DTI's Role

Trevor Holley is a Chartered Mechanical Engineer. He served his apprenticeship at Woolwich Arsenal, worked for the Ministry of Supply at the Atomic Energy Authority Plants at Risley, Windscale and at Aldermarston, and worked for the Ministry of Defence at ordnance factories and at the headquarters in South London. He moved to the Ministry of Technology in 1969, and is now a Principal Professional and Technology Officer at the DTI with responsibility for two sections. One covers machinery for plastics; rubber and leather working; tanning; boot, shoe and brush making; cable making and wire winding; and fluid power equipment. The other is responsible for machinery for textiles; garment making; laundry and dry cleaning; tufted carpets; matress-making and sewing machines. It sounds a somewhat disparate collection of industrial sectors, and Holley would not demur from that. A few years ago, when staffing levels were higher, he would have responsibility for fewer sectors, and so be better able to become involved with them. He still keeps in touch with the major personalities and likes to be aware of the trading situation of companies at home and abroad. But his profile is inevitably lower than once it was.

Trevor Holley learned of the potential Shelley Thermoformers project because he knew Leslie Perryman: although he does not specialise in MAP applications like some Project Officers, the case would have come before him because of his sponsoring role for the plastics machinery industry. The application having been received in mid-December, Holley and Trevor Gilpin visited the company on 16 January to assess the situation. Present for Shelley were Leslie Perryman and Electrical Design Manager, Bill Farrant: Nigel Smith of Modus Systems, the consultants, were also there. The report of that vital meeting is classified "Commercial in Confidence" and is not made available to the applicant, but it is useful to consider here what areas it covers.

The report describes Shelley Thermoformers as the leading UK manufacturer in its field and notes the stimulating effect of the Andrew Deacon takeover – particularly with regard to exports. Turnover and employment is discussed, and the workings of a thermoformer are described in simple terms. The company's main competitors – mostly from overseas – are listed, and it is noted that "all these companies already offer machines fitted with varying degrees of microprocessor control".

The features of the proposed microelectronics application are then described – again in layman's terms – and the suitability of Modus Systems to help in the project is confirmed. From a tour of the plant the report says "we saw several large machines in course of construction for a number of overseas countries, including customers in Korea and Nigeria, and a generally fully occupied workforce bore witness to the strong order book". The concluding remarks are: "The decision to proceed with the development of microprocessor based control systems is essential for the future prosperity of the company. Mr Gilpin and the writer are satisfied that the MAP project is sound and worthwhile. The acquisition of the company by the Deacon Group is welcomed and the consequent appointment of the new director whose prime function is the development of exports should help to consolidate and expand the growing emphasis on overseas business. An encouraging visit. The company should be watched with interest".

From this report was drawn up the MAP Case Paper which – although more formally laid out – arrives at similar conclusions. "Technically this appears to be a sound development. The consultants appear to be highly competent and this programme of work should certainly be within their capabilities. The technology transfer has been fully considered and Shelley Thermoformers should end up considerably more advanced, microelectronically, at the conclusion of the project. I would therefore recommend support for the applicant on technical grounds."

This report was put to the next meeting of the MAP Executive Committee on 23 February, two months after the application was received and one month after the site visit. The Executive Committee – made up of officials from Electronics Applications Division with a departmental accountant – considered a varied collection of applications that morning with Shelley Thermoformers being squeezed between applications for a microcomputer based central heating controller and a multi-channel continuous flow analyser. An agreement in principle was given and 'phoned to Leslie Perryman that day, but there was a problem with the accountants.

To qualify for a grant, a company has to prove "additionality" – that is, that the project would not have gone ahead in that form or in that timescale without support. The DTI's Accountancy Services Division presented a five-page report on 12 March concluding "we consider that there is no case for additionality due to financial constraint". The company was felt to be doing too well to warrant support.

This was not the end of the story! Trevor Holley asked Shelley Thermoformers for more information to support the company's claim, and a revised cash flow prediction was sent on 25 March. The following week some evidence of the strength of foreign competition was provided in the form of internal minutes recording lost orders. Holley asked for the decision on "additionality" to be reconsidered, and the DTI accountants gave their verdict on 6 April. Swayed particularly by the financial constraints caused by an imminent move to new premises with higher overheads, they agreed that "the company's case on additionality is reasonable".

On 9 April Trevor Holley wrote to the MAP executive, asking if the project could now be supported: an affirmative reply is dated the same day. The company was informed, and a letter setting out all the terms and conditions of the 25 per cent support was sent on behalf of the Secretary of State on 15 April.

The terms of a MAP grant inevitably include a number of provisions – most significantly for Trevor Holley's duties the provision that each claim for payment must be accompanied by a report covering various aspects. Holley must vouch that this report is acceptable, and so he obviously needs to keep in touch.

But at any one time, Holley's section may have 40 projects such as this progressing through it, and there are duties beyond dealing with applications. Briefing on policy issues, preparing answers to Parliamentary Questions and liaising with research associations are among the claims on Holley's time. So his involvement with Shelley Thermoformers and companies in similar positions is kept to a minimum. Higher risk projects may be visited after each quarterly report, but most would be seen at the half-way stage and again at the end.

Trevor Holley admits to getting "a great deal of satisfaction when a company pulls it off. We see people in the office or at their plant who have no idea of what to expect from the Civil Service. They are pleased to find that we speak their language and can understand what they are doing, and we usually enjoy working together. But not every story is a success. We do have to turn companies down, and projects can prove troublesome. Obviously we do all we can to help but – in the last resort – our responsibility is to the government and the taxpayer: it is not to a firm in trouble."

We began by saying that the story of a MAP application would lack the ingredients of the Canterbury Tales, but it may be that an applicant could apply Chaucer's words to his Project Officer "he loved chivalrie, throuthe and honour, freedom and curteisie".

CONCLUSION

WILLIAM PLOWDEN

This book, and the seminar which gave rise to it, is addressed to a particular aspect of a general problem. The general problem is the extreme difficulty which many people in Britain experience in trying to understand the ways in which central government works. Who does what, and how, and who should take credit or blame for specific policy decisions? For many people the television series *Yes, Minister* confirmed the view which they already held that for much of the time nobody is really in control; but that for most of the rest of the time the Civil Service determines the course steered, with ministers from time to time giving a rather random push to the tiller.

Very funny though this can be made to seem, it is less funny when in real life those outside government start to wonder how they can influence decisions and policies. They would be better able to do so if they knew more about the ways the wheels go round. But government, like many other institutions in Britain, has traditionally been a very private business. Ministerial memoirs, notably Richard Crossman's, have occasionally shed light on the subject, but usually conceal more than they reveal. Civil servants, the central subject of this book, who know more about the workings of central government than anybody else, have adopted reticence as one of their primary professional virtues. This posture has been reinforced by the Official Secrets Acts. Outsiders have not always been eager to learn; even those who grumble about the incompetence of government are often oddly incurious about the reasons for it.

The particular aspect of the problem is, of course, that industry – using that term to mean the whole of the commercial sector – is as badly informed as anybody else. In a much-governed society such as Britain, such ignorance is a disability for any sectoral interest; it is of wider significance when the interest concerned is, in theory, the mainspring of the economy and the main source of wealth on which all the rest of us – including government – depend.

Wyn Grant puts it nicely in his concluding remarks in chapter 8 of this book:

. . . In a democratic society, the views of government and business are not always going to coincide, but what is important is that each side should have an understanding of the other's perspectives, decision-making mechanisms and problems. . . . If better mutual understandings could be created, then in the long run we would certainly all be better off."

At least two aims are served by giving "each side" a better understanding of the other. First, and most obviously, this greatly helps the efficient communication of messages of all kinds, in both directions. Governments trying to market a new service or to persuade industry to act in particular ways must, for a start, know to whom to address themselves and in what language to speak. (The peculiar written language of Whitehall, with its elegant shadings and qualifications, can completely baffle those who do not normally use it.) Firms, reciprocally, with a request or a problem need to know whereabouts in Whitehall (or elsewhere) to turn, and at which level in the hierarchy.

More broadly, there is often such a wide gap, in attitudes, experience and objectives, between industry and government that misunderstandings and friction are disturbingly easy. Why don't firms respond as anticipated to schemes of industrial assistance? Why do government departments take so long to reply to urgent requests from firms, and why are civil servants so chary about treating exceptional cases exceptionally? (There is a muted but very clear echo of these themes in Nigel East's interesting account of what seems otherwise to have been a mutually satisfactory relationship.) Underlying these specific niggles is the fundamental difference of attitude, well illustrated by Sir Kenneth Corfield in chapter 10 between those whose professional lives revolve around risks and rewards (and are often lived in places remote from London SW1) and those whose job satisfaction derives from playing the complex but in personal terms risk-free game of three-dimensional chess which can be offered by work in democratic government (the end-game of which often takes place in or within a mile of the Palace of Westminster – despite John Bourn's useful reminder that very many civil servants work neither in offices nor in London).

The problem, of course, is that, as Dr. Grant points out, governments cannot, and should not, always do what industry would like them to. In a democracy, even one in industrial decline, resources have to be devoted to activities other than industrial development : public health, income maintenance, the arts. Other interests must be accommodated : preserving the environment, protecting consumers, maintaining free trade, are legitimate tasks for governments but can give headaches to industry. So too, incidentally, can actions by government which protect or strengthen the position of the workforce. It is perhaps characteristically British that the term 'industry', in this book as elsewhere, usually means 'industrial management'. Management deals with the industrial departments in Whitehall; workers deal with the labour departments. The National Economic Development Council and its supporting bodies are almost unique in bringing government and both sides of industry together round the same table as a matter of course. The process of accommodation leads to both delays and outcomes which are often at the bottom of industry's complaints about the unhelpful attitudes of government. Almost any change of policy leads to complaints, as witness the chorus that greeted the government's proposals in November 1984 to revise its regional assistance policy. But it would be nice to think that such changes were made with full understanding of their impact on industry, as on other interests. This is not always so.

Two sharply contrasting themes, one explicit, one implicit, run through much of this book. The explicit theme is *change*. Sir Edward du Cann on the new Select Committees, Anne Mueller on the Department of Trade and Industry's efforts to clarify its objectives, Peter Le Cheminant on the government's Efficiency Unit and the Financial Management Initiative, Dennis Trevelyan on new developments in training, are all at pains to emphasise that things are changing in Westminster and Whitehall and in the relationship between them. Industry, as the client and sometimes critic of government, is assured that government is improving its organisation, skills and performance.

The other theme, less obvious but all-pervasive, is *continuity*. The Civil Service, like other British institutions, took broadly its modern form at the highwater point of Britain's recent history. Many of its characteristics date from the period of its reform during the last quarter of the nineteenth century. (This was, ironically, the period which saw the beginning of Britain's long slow industrial decline which is the backdrop to the whole of this book.) Much the same is true of the structure of government; perhaps the last major innovation was the creation of the Cabinet secretariat in 1916. Parliament, too, Select Committees apart, is in many ways a nineteenth century institution. Its procedures, as Sir Edward du Cann points out, are in large part quite unsuited to dealing with the problems and responsibilities of modern government. John Bourn's account of the large size and formal structure of the Civil Service prompts the thought that such an organisation must be slow to change. My own view is that such an organisation must – understandably – be slow even to accept the need for change. Sir Kenneth Corfield sees the problem of change, or its absence, as even more widely based : he points to various recent small-scale changes in the government-industry relationship but concludes, rather pessimistically in my opinion, that fundamental changes can be only part of a very long-term process of changing social attitudes – which in turn requires a major reorientation of the educational system. He may well be right; but in that kind of time-scale we shall all be dead.

One topic about which it might have been helpful to hear more is the role of politics, and politicians, in the whole process. It may seem perverse to demand this of a book about the Civil Service. But the work of civil servants is influenced by, and filtered through, ministers, in ways that are much more blurred and ambiguous than those described either in constitutional textbooks or in politicians' memoirs. My own view is that the professional reticence of the Civil Service allows it often to be cast as scapegoat and portrayed as wholly to blame for decisions for which ministers – vacillating, short-sighted or simply incompetent – are at least partly responsible. It is ironic in the 1980s to see civil servants lambasted as inadequate managers by politicians many of whom have managed nothing more complex than their constituency surgery. The relationships between civil servants and ministers need more analysis and are probably overdue for change.

In general, though, the right outcome in Whitehall is probably a blend of change and continuity. The first step is better understanding of existing arrangements. If we are to make sensible decisions about which features of British government are worth keeping and which should be consigned to the dustbin, it will be very important to have constructive criticism not only from insiders and specialist experts in government but from anyone with relevant experience to offer. The private sector of industry certainly does not have all the answers, but it knows quite a lot about the problems. This book ought to help it to aim its comments a good deal more accurately.

APPENDICES

GOVERNMENT INFORMATION FOR INDUSTRY

Introduction

APPENDIX 1

APPENDIX 2

APPENDIX 3

APPENDIX 4

APPENDIX 5

INTRODUCTION

The main text of *Today's Civil Service* is concerned with the working of the Civil Service generally, its relationship with Parliament and its particular relationship with industry – the latter seen from the viewpoint both of industry and of the Civil Service. It concludes with a case study of the Civil Service and industry working together.

The appendices which follow aim to continue this practical aspect of the book by setting down the objectives, structure and the detailed organisation and services of the government department most involved in working with industry. Two further appendices describe the essential publications and statistics of Government which are especially concerned with the industrial sector.

The importance of the role of government vis à vis industry is a fact, whatever the view of the political masters of the day, and it is essential to grasp the system in order to use it. This is especially important for the industrialist, the potential investor, the local councillor and official, the members and staff of countless boards, etc. that link the Whitehall decision and the individual citizen together with those wishing to start new businesses or preserve established ones. And there are also those who support these decision makers, their special advisers, researchers, the industrial libraries and the trade associations, etc.

It is hoped then that these appendices will help the reader to establish and relate his needs to the organisation of government and lead him to the right address, telephone number or publication so he may secure the necessary Government information.

To ensure accuracy and currency appendices 1–4 have been prepared within the Department of Trade and Industry while appendix 5 has been prepared by a member of the staff of the House of Commons Library whose job, on behalf of Members, is to act as statistical information broker between government and Parliament.

A rather detailed table of contents is designed to elucidate quickly the information in the appendices. The guide to the Department of Trade and Industry in appendix 3 is based on the April 1985 edition of the DTI Guide which is published twice yearly in *British business* (enquiries 01-211 6074). appendix 4 was prepared by the Department of Trade and Industry Library services.

APPENDIX 1

Government Sponsorship of Industry

Introduction

The function of government, called 'industrial sponsorship' has two main aims. These are first to ensure that the views and interests of industry in Britain are known to and understood by those in government who make and apply policies, which have any bearing, direct or indirect, on the operations of industry and secondly to attempt to ensure that the concerns of government are understood by industry.

The need for such a government function arises from the nature of modern industrial society. There are three principal justifications:-

i Britain, like all developed western countries, has a mixed economy. Government spending represents a very substantial proportion of our Gross Domestic Product. Even if government did not choose to manipulate the economic conditions in which industry operated, its own basic operations, would still have substantial implications for industry of which government needs to be aware. Public purchasing policy is an obvious example.

ii Government takes an active role often involving protective or regulatory legislation in pursuit of objectives, few of them primarily directed at industry, but where the application of policy may nonetheless have substantial implications for industry; environmental policy, local planning policies and employment protection legislation are examples. Again, the implications for industry must be understood and taken into account.

iii The basic financial activities of industry have always been regarded as appropriate or convenient media for the levying of taxes.

The operation of government thus clearly has a major impact on both the general environment in which industry operates and on the particular activities of particular businesses. It is for this reason that it is nowadays assumed, almost as a commonplace, that there must be people in government who "know about" or "deal with" each individual industry. The need originally emerged during the two world wars when control of production and resources created a need for understanding within government of industry, its operations and its needs and lead to the creation of structures and organisations which could provide this. Between the wars and with the move away from detailed regulation in the years after the Second World War, this role declined in importance. The need for it was recognised again in the early/mid 1960s, when the sponsorship function as it is currently carried out began to emerge.

What is Sponsorship?

Essentially, for any identifiable sector of industry, there will be a government department which assumes "sponsorship" responsibility and within that department there will be a person or unit with special sponsorship responsibility. The sponsor will generally try to maintain a reasonable level of understanding of the sector, its particular characteristics, its markets, its major companies and its representative organs, usually trade associations. The sponsors of particular sectors will vary in their involvement: in the depth of their contacts, in the amount of information they find it necessary to have readily available and so on. All, however, will expect to be consulted by their colleagues in government on policy or legislative proposals likely to have a significant bearing on their sector of industry and all will be expected to keep a weather-eye open for implications arising from such legislation and changes. They will be used by colleagues as a sounding board for preliminary proposals and will either advise on or carry out consultations, formal or informal at the stage when this becomes appropriate. Within their departments they will usually be seen as the advocates of their industry, just as their departments often will be within goverment as a whole, though the industry concerned may very well see them only as the apologists of government.

How does it work?

On general topics the sponsor will usually act, with the trade association, as the channel through which concern or representation about policies are transmitted to government and, vice versa, as one of the means by which government attempts to consult, to explain and justify its policies and transmit its own needs and priorities.

Apart from contacts at the representative level via trade associations, sponsors also often deal direct with individual firms. In particular the DTI's programme of Support for Innovation has been administered by the sponsor divisions of that Department.

Generally, though, on broader questions relating to the implications of government policy, individual firms should make their enquiries via their trade associations, who will be better able to direct enquiries to the right person at the right level.

Who sponsors what?

The sponsorship function traditionally has related primarily to manufacturing industry and it is in this field that it is most fully developed. In other sectors arrangements are less straightforward. In broad outline, the responsibilities are:-

Industry	**Department**
Agriculture, forestry fisheries	Ministry of Agriculture, Fisheries and Food, Scottish Office, Welsh Office, Northern Ireland Office.
Extractive industries	
Oil, coal and gas	Dept of Energy
Other	Dept of Trade and Industry
Manufacturing industry	Dept of Trade and Industry except:-
Building materials	Dept of the Environment
Defence equipment	Ministry of Defence
Food	Ministry of Agriculture, Fisheries and Food
Medical equipment and pharmaceuticals	Dept of Health and Social Security
Construction industry	Dept of the Environment
Distribution, hotels, tourism, publishing, films	Dept of Trade and Industry
Transport industry	Dept of Transport
Communications industries	Dept of Trade and Industry
Financial, insurance and other business services	Dept of Trade and Industry

Responsibilities within the DTI are set out in more detail in the guide at appendix 3.

APPENDIX 2

The Department of Trade and Industry: Strategic Aims

Introduction

In early 1984, the DTI published its Strategic Aims. These were "to encourage, assist, and ensure the proper regulation of, British trade, industry and commerce; to increase the growth of world trade and the national production of wealth". Subsidiary aims were set out under four headings.

A Climate

1 A financial and fiscal climate which encourages enterprise, investment and growth and minimises government burdens on business.

2 A wider understanding of the value of productive activity, enterprise and profit.

3 European Community and international agreements, laws and commercial relations working to the advantage of UK trade and investment.

4 A regulatory framework which promotes fair competition and the efficient use of resources and safeguards the interests of customers.

5 Standards which strengthen the international competitiveness of British trade, industry and commerce.

6 Reduced UK regional disparities.

B International Competitiveness

1 Improved management and other skills throughout UK industry and commerce, targetting smaller firms in particular.

2 Market information and support for UK firms competing in overseas markets.

3 Increased efficiency in state owned enterprises through privatisation, exposure to competition, target setting and monitoring.

4 Inward investment and collaboration with foreign companies yielding advantages to the UK.

5 Measures to increase UK output, improve performance and encourage the formation of new businesses.

C Innovation

1 Increased civil R&D in industry.

2 Effective exploitation of UK and foreign science and technology.

3 Awareness and rapid adoption of key technologies.

4 Levels of quality and design to the highest world standards.

5 Closer co-operation on new products between UK producers and customers, for example through public purchasing.

D DTI Management Task

To use departmental resources efficiently to pursue these aims.

These aims were accompanied by the following statement which explains the thinking behind them and shows some of the ways in which they will be achieved.

I Why aims?

DTI has the task of helping British firms to compete successfully for customers at home and abroad. It employs nearly 13,000 people and is responsible for government spending of some £1400 million a year. Any organisation accounting for resources of this magnitude needs a clear view of its central purpose and objectives if time, effort and money are to be used to best effect.

The statement of its aims shows in a concise form the Department's main purpose. The central aim is to encourage, assist, and ensure the proper regulation of, British trade, industry and commerce: to increase the growth of world trade and the national production of wealth. This will be achieved in three main ways, by promoting:

a **climate** for British industry and commerce which is as conducive to enterprise and competition as that in any other industrialised country

the **international competitiveness** of British firms through increased efficiency and adaptability

Innovation to improve the products, processes and services that British industry and commerce can offer to the world.

Under these three headings there is a series of subsidiary aims. These individual aims define in a relatively simple way the principal tasks required to make progress towards the achievement of the central aim.

II Climate, International Competitiveness, and Innovation

Climate
The right climate is vital to the achievement of our central aim. Without it, enterprising people with new ideas will be unable to create wealth and new jobs. First, business needs a stable financial and fiscal regime if it is to have confidence to innovate and invest. Inflation must be reduced and eventually eliminated and public expenditure must be strictly controlled to keep down taxes and help moderate interest rates. It means the removal of unnecessary burdens, the improvement of incentives, giving better returns for effort and enterprise, and the encouragement of financial institutions able to satisfy the needs of large and small firms alike. In this area, the DTI works closely with the Treasury and other departments to ensure that the needs of industry and commerce are taken fully into account when the priorities for government action are decided (Aim A.1). The Department also works with organisations in the education field and elsewhere to make the value of productive activity more widely understood, and to emphasise that wealth must be generated before it can be used (A.2).

Second, business needs proper access to overseas markets. For a major trading nation, exporting nearly 30% of its output, international barriers and distortions to trade are a major threat to the generation of wealth. Removing these burdens requires constant work at government to government level, particularly in the face of pressures for protection arising from economic and debt problems around the world. The Department represents the UK's industrial and commercial interests in the European Community, in other international organisations, and in a wide range of bilateral relationships (A.3). This work helps companies to export successfully and underpins the Department's direct export promotion work (B.2).

Third, a regulatory framework is needed to enable the market to function effectively: a framework of company and competition law. The Department also has responsibilities for the consumer, and for safety legislation. The right balance has to be struck between too much regulation, which stifles enterprise, and too little regulation, which can lead to injustice, uncertainty, or erosion of competition in the market place (A.4). The Department is also concerned to strengthen the British standards system and encourage the widest possible use of standards by both buyers and sellers. A strong standards system promotes quality and customer confidence at home and overseas (A.5).

Finally, an effective regional policy can help ease social change and reduce disparities in employment opportunities. The 1983 White Paper on Regional Industrial Development (Cmnd 9111) outlines a new and more cost-effective approach, within which the Department will work, with industry, to promote new business and new jobs in the assisted areas, in both manufacturing and services (A.6).

Competitiveness

The Department's aims under this heading are directed to ensuring that British companies have the tools they need to meet and beat international competition, not least skilled workers of every grade. Proper skills are vital and the DTI works with other agencies to help improve training and increase the industrial and commercial relevance of education at all levels. It has a special interest in the improvement of management skills and under the Department's Small Firms Service (see p.155) experienced businessmen advise owners and managers of small businesses, and those thinking of starting their own businesses, on their plans and problems (B.1).

The British Overseas Trade Board (see p.143) whose members are mainly businessmen, directs the Department's export promotion programme. Its staff in the UK and the commercial staff in embassies and consulates overseas provide advice and information to exporter and would-be exporters and practical and financial help with entry into new markets. The Department's Projects and Export Policy Division co-ordinates all forms of Government assistance for major project contracts overseas. The Exports Credits Guarantee Department (see p.156) provides a wide range of credit insurance and related services for exporters (B.2).

For those large areas of economic activity in the public sector privatisation provides a special opportunity to increase competitiveness by exposure to market forces. The liberalisation of the telecommunications market and the privatisation of British Telecom are designed to stimulate new mass industries in communications and office services. The disciplines now imposed on state-owned firms already exposed to competition, such as BL and Rolls Royce have led to major improvements in competitiveness and brought them closer to readiness for return to the private sector (B.3).

Investment in the UK by foreign-owned companies can bring many benefits, both in terms of output and jobs and through the spreading of new management styles and attitudes, and of quality, standards and technology. The UK can offer the overseas investor EC membership, a worldwide reputation for inventiveness and intellect, and a highly developed and efficient infrastructure and services sector. The Invest in Britain Bureau (see p.138) co-ordinates promotional work to bring further inward investment to the UK. Recent examples include the decisions by the Finnish firm United Paper Mills to set up a pulp and newsprint mill in Clwyd and by American computer companies Digital and Hewlett Packard to establish research and development facilities in southern England (B.4).

The Department runs a number of other schemes designed to support increased efficiency and adaptability in British firms. For example, in conjunction with the banks it operates the Loan Guarantee Scheme to help small businesses obtain loan finance. Selective financial assistance is also available for major investment projects providing positive benefits for the economy (B.5).

Innovation

Industrial and commercial innovation is vital if Britain is to maintain and increase its share of world markets. This requires increased spending by industry and commerce on market-related research and development for civil purposes. Through the Department's Support for Innovation programme companies can receive assistance both for longer term R&D projects designed to strengthen their technological base and for development work on new and improved products and processes (C.1).

The UK has a good record in basic research, but the creation of wealth depends upon the profitable exploitation by industry and commerce of the fruits of this research and of science and technology developed overseas (B.2). As well as running the Patent Office (see p.139), an important link in the chain from idea to commercial realisation, the Department runs four major industrial research establishments which identify, develop and transfer to industry new technologies with widespread applications. The Department is co-ordinating a major national research effort in advanced information technology the Alvey programme (see p.142). It also provides a number of information services to help companies identify scientific and technological opportunities available to them both at home and abroad.

The last few years have seen the emergence of major new technologies such as Microelectronics, Information Technology, Biotechnology and Advanced Manufacturing Technology which offer opportunities across a wide swathe of industry and commerce. Only by the acquisition of new skills and techniques will firms be able to maximise opportunities to create new wealth. The awareness and rapid adoption of these key technologies (C.3) have been promoted by the Department through special measures within the Support for Innovation programme covering awareness, training, consultancy and project support.

Design is a crucial element in the successful development of new products. Good design combines what customers want with what is commercially and technically possible, and concentration on better quality during the manufacturing process can also yield significant returns for companies. The Department draws the attention of managers throughout industry to the importance of design and quality (C.4). In addition, small and medium sized companies can get both free and subsidised consultancy on these subjects.

Firms which are successful innovators are able to link their technological expertise to a knowledge of the market. Closer cooperation between UK producers and their customers (C.5) is one way of ensuring that new products meet the needs of the market. The Department encourages public sector purchasers to give a lead in collaborating with their suppliers on their future needs. One example of this is in office automation where twenty pilot projects have been set up and are now under evaluation with many valuable lessons for suppliers and users alike.

The aims in Management

The aims form the backdrop against which the day-to-day work of the Department is conducted and progress assessed. The Department's own 'management task' is to ensure that the resources available are used as efficiently and effectively as possible in the achievement of these aims. Each division now draws up its own policy objectives in support of the aims and where possible is set quantified targets against which progress can be measured. Objectives, targets and progress towards them will be reviewed each year by senior management and Ministers to ensure the Department remains on course. This will help to identify and overcome at an early stage failures to achieve intended progress, as well as activities which have served their purposes or are ineffective, so that the resources can be redeployed to other necessary tasks or simply saved.

APPENDIX 3

The Department of Trade and Industry: A Guide

The Department of Trade and Industry has a broad ranging field of responsibilities:-

a *Overseas Trade*: International trade policy, including promotion of UK trade interests in the European Communities, General Agreement on Tariffs and Trade, Organisation for Economic Corporation and Development, UNCTAD and other international organisations;

b *Export Promotion*: Under the direction of the British Overseas Trade Board (see p.143), the promotion of UK exports and assistance to exporters;

c *Industrial Policy and Assistance*: Policy in relation to industry, including promotion of the interests of industry and assistance to industry; specific interests in all manufacturing and service industries apart from those covered by other departments (see p.128); regional policy and regional industrial assistance (some of this applying only to England); policy towards small firms; and policy in relation to public bodies for which the Department is responsible – British Ship Builders, British Steel Corporation, The Post Office and the British Technology Group;

d *Competition and Consumer Affairs*: Competition policy and consumer protection, including relations with the Office of Fair Trading and the Monopolies and Mergers Commission, and the National Weights and Measures Laboratory;

e *Science, Technology and Research*: Policy on science and technology and research and development matters, standards and designs, support for innovation and the administration of the National Physical Laboratory (see p.140), the National Engineering Laboratory (see p.140), Warren Spring Laboratory (see p.140) and the Laboratory of the Government Chemist (see p.141);

f *Company Legislation, Radio Frequencies, Patents*: Administration of company legislation and Companies Registration Office (see p.142); insolvency service; regulation of the insurance industry; regulation of radio frequencies; and Patent Office (see p.139).

g *Statistics*: The Business Statistics Office (See p.146).

I Headquarters Structure

The Civil Service organisation of the Department of Trade and Industry is headed by a Permanent Secretary, in early 1985 Sir Brian Hayes. Eleven Deputy Secretaries report to him, each responsible for a group of organisational units called a division. The divisions are grouped into "line" divisions, with direct responsibility for advice on policy or the management of departmental functions (Numbers 1–30 below) and "services" divisions providing general management services and support to the Department (Numbers 31–41 below). This structure follows and the London address of each Division is indicated by a bracketed code at the end of each entry. A key to these codes is given at the end of this section. An index to the responsibilities listed can be found on p.148.

1 Regional policy. Regional industrial policy. Designation of assisted areas and derelict land clearance areas. Provision of government funded factories and offices in England (through English Estates). Organisation and functions of the department's regional offices and liaison with related divisions of the Scottish Office, Welsh Office and Department of Economic Development in Northern Ireland. European Community regional policy, including assistance from the European regional development fund, Business Improvement Services policy on regional development grants under the Industrial Development Act 1982. Selective financial assistance for manufacturing and service industries under section 7 of the Industrial Development Act 1982. Promotion of assisted areas. (K).

Regional Development Grant Offices

Billingham
Department of Trade and Industry, Regional Development Grants Office, Queensway House, West Precinct, Billingham, Cleveland TS23 2NF. Tel (0642) 553671. Telex: 58608. Answer back: 58608 RDG BIL G.
Area for which responsible: those parts of the following counties that have special development area or development area status Cleveland, Cumbria, Durham, Humberside, Lincolnshire, Northumberland, North Yorkshire, South Yorkshire, Tyne and Wear.

Bootle
Department of Trade and Industry, Regional Development Grants Office, St Peter's House, Stanley Precinct, Bootle, Merseyside L20 3LZ. Tel 051–922 4030. Telex 627162. Answer back: 627162 RDG BOT G.
Area for which responsible: those parts of the following counties that have special development area or development area status: Cheshire, Greater Manchester, Lancashire, Merseyside, Northamptonshire.

Cardiff
Department of Trade and Industry, Regional Development Grants Office, 24–26 Newport Road, Cardiff CF2 1SY. Tel (0222) 492611. Telex 498538. Answer back: 498538 RDG CAR G.
Area for which responsible: those parts of Wales, Cornwall (including the Isles of Scilly) and Devon that have special development area or development area status.

Glasgow
Department of Trade and Industry, Regional Development Grants Office, Magnet House, 59 Waterloo Street, Glasgow G2 7BT. Tel 041–221 9833. Telex 777911. Answer back: 777911 RDG GLA G.
Area for which responsible: those parts of Scotland that have special development area or development area status.

Assisted Areas: November 1984

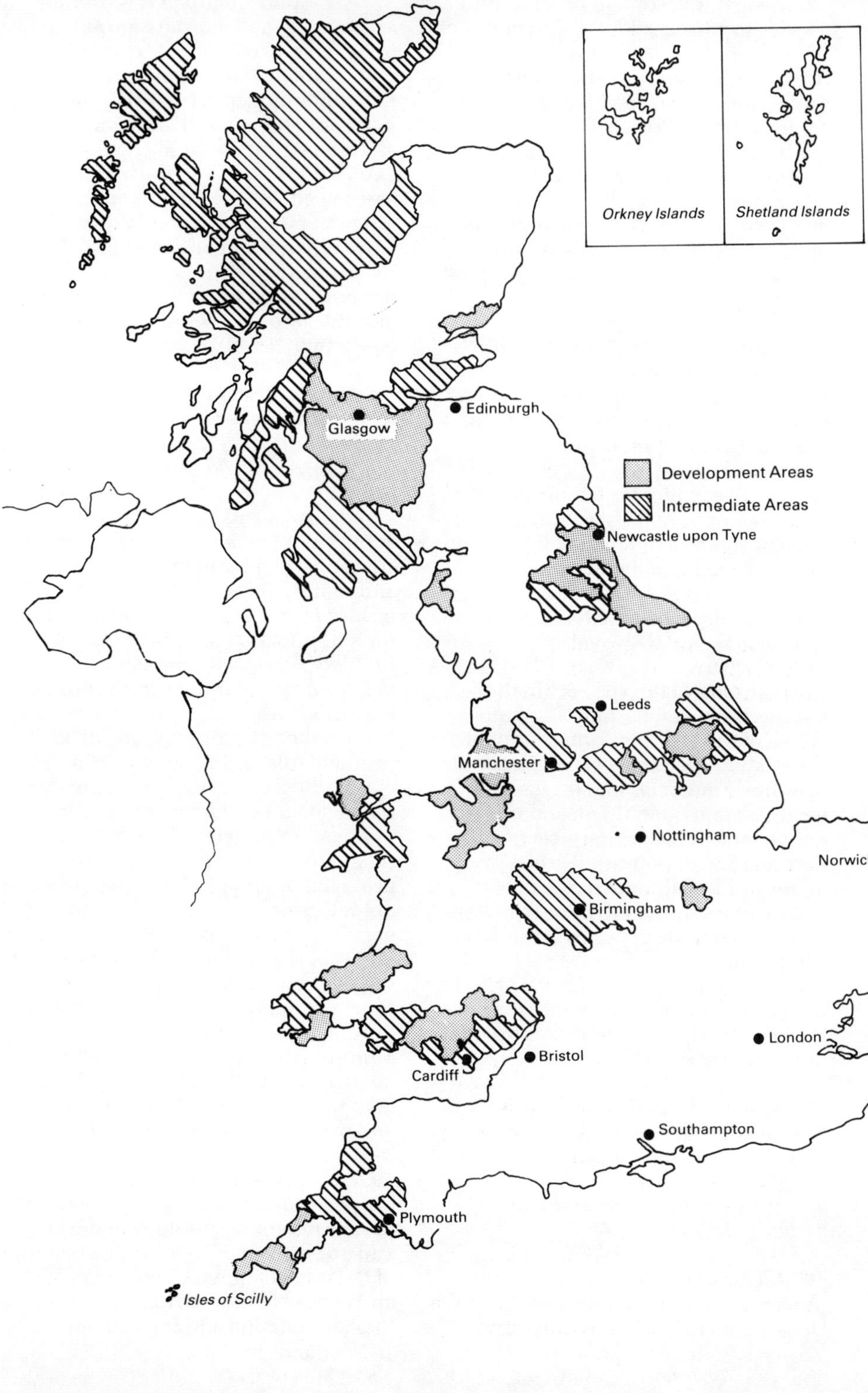

2 Inward investment, tourism and service industries. Promotion of direct investment from abroad into the UK (Invest in Britain Bureau). Tourism policy and project assistance, sponsorship of British Tourist Authority, English Tourist Board and the hotel industry and liaison with travel trade. Sponsorship of printing and publishing industries. Sponsorship of the distributive trades (excluding food and drink) and certain high street service trades. (K).

3 Small firms. Focal point within government where the needs of small firms, including cooperatives, are seen as a whole. Continuous review of their place in the national economy to ensure that small firms' interests are taken into account in the formulation of government policies. Administration of the loan guarantee scheme. Focal point for contact and cooperation with local entrprise agencies. Central management of the small firms service (see p. 155) (ASH).

4 Radio regulatory. Coordination of UK interests, and participation on behalf of the UK, in all international negotiations on the use and allocation of radio frequencies and on the technical and operating standards for radiocommunication services. Formulation of policy governing the planning allocation of frequencies to all radio services in the UK. Licensing of non-Crown users of radio; formulation of equipment performance specifications and of technical criteria to be observed. Enforcement of the Wireless Telegraphy Acts; control of interference. (WBH).

5 Industrial development unit. National financial assistance under section 8 of the Industrial Development Act 1982. Appraisal of major applications for selective financial assistance. (K).

6 Accountancy services. A professional accountancy service to the Department of Trade and Industry.

7 Air. Sponsorship of the aircraft, aero-engine and aircraft equipment industries. Government investment in civil aircraft, aero-engine and helicopter projects. International matters in the aircraft, aero-engine and aircraft equipment fields, including export questions. Technical and market assessment of current and future civil aircraft and air transport systems. Aircraft environmental matters. Research and technology demonstration programmes on civil aircraft, aero-engines and aircraft equipment. (VA).

8 Electronics applications. Responsibility for the encouragement of electronic, particularly microelectronic, applications in UK industry. Sponsorship of the computer aided design and automatic test equipment vendor industry, electronic component, instrumentation and automation industries, including industrial automation systems and their application to industrial problems, the water industry, electronic point of sale and vending machines, weighing machines, amusement machines, video disks, visual displays, and scientific, medical, bio-medical and optical instruments. Management of the microelectronics application project (Map), the microelectronics industry support programme (Misp), the fibre optics and optoelectronics scheme (Fos), the electronics computer-aided design, manufacture and test scheme (Cadmat), the joint optoelectronics research scheme (Joers), and the secretariat of the electronics and avionics requirements board including its control electronics and instruments committee and the advanced devices and materials committee. (BP).

9 Information technology. Responsibility for the encouragement of information technology and its use and application in the UK. Sponsorship of the information technology industry and of the electronics industry (other than automation and instruments), including the computer industry (hardware and software); telecommunications; electronic consumer and capital goods; broadcasting equipment, and office equipment. (BP).

10 Space, the Post Office and films. Industrial space policy and sponsorship of the space industry. UK delegation to the European Space Agency. Sponsorship and government oversight of the Post Office including National Girobank. Coordination of the department's policy on nationalised industries. International postal relations (inc. EC) involving government interests. Universal Postal Union (UPU). Conference of European Posts and Telecommunications (Cept) and Conference of Commonwealth Postal Administrations (CCPA). General questions of legislation affecting the Post Office including philatelic questions. Government oversight of private courier services. Sponsorship and regulation of the film industry. (BP).

11 Telecommunications. Granting of licences under the Telecommunications Act 1984 and the implementation of the liberalisation awareness programme under it. Sponsorship of British Telecommunications plc, Cable and Wireless plc, Mercury Communications Ltd, value added network service providers, cellular radio network operators and the telecommunications manufacturing industry. Promotion of telecoms exports. Teletex scheme. Governmental aspects of international telecommunications relations including International Telecommunication Union, Conference of European Posts and Telecommunications (Cept), European Community Commonwealth Tele-communications Organisation, Intelsat, Eutelsat and Inmarsat matters. (V).

12 Quality and education. Development of better understanding of the role of industry and commerce, and better preparation of individuals for industrial/commercial careers via industry/education links. Promotion of business appreciation, entrepreneurial spirit, technology in schools and relevant engineering in higher education. Encouragement of the development of skills relevant to the needs of industry in the most cost effective way and departmental interest in industrial training. Sponsorship of Engineering Council, British Schools Technology (BST), Science and Technology Regional Organisations (Satros) and Information Technology Centres (ITeCs). Promotion of technology transfer from academic institutions to industry and vice versa. Sponsorship of British Technology Group (BTG) new university/industry partnerships, and technical information and data services for industry. Development of government policy on quality, design standards and certification. Sponsorship of British Standards Institution (BSI), Institute of Quality Assurance (IQA) and the National Accreditation Council. Promotion of improved industrial performance and the formulation of design, quality, management, education, and marketing policies. Management of business and technical advisory services, such as management advisory service, design advisory service funded consultancy scheme, small firms technical inquiry service, quality assurance advisory service. Coordination of UK interests in eliminating technical barriers to trade (mainly through EC and GATT) and representation at international standards fora.

13 Patent Office and industrial property and copyright department. The establishment and protection of intellectual property rights including the grant of patents and the registration of industrial designs and trade marks. Legislation and domestic and international policy on the matters including copyright. (Sub-office at Baskerville House, Browncross Street, New Bailey Street, Salford M3 5FU, tel 061–832 9571 for trade marks and designs only). (P).

14 Research and technology policy. Advice on general science and technology policy and on coordination of R&D resources. Studies on policy, organisation and long-term strategy. Coordination of Departmental support of R&D programmes. Central coordination of matters affecting the research establishments. Information on overseas science and technology. Exploitation of the work of scientific counsellors at UK posts overseas. International science and technology agreements. Implementation of technological collaboration agreements between the UK and other countries: assisting in technological exchanges. European Community R&D programmes. Departmental interests in research councils and environmental issues, and research in universities, nationalised industries, and other departments. Operation of teaching company scheme (with Serc), and visiting engineers scheme. Sponsorship of the research associations and other major R&D contractors to the department. Responsibility for metrology and standards requirements board. (ASH).

Requirements boards. The Department of Trade and Industry's research and development requirements boards advise on the objectives, composition and balance of the DTI research and technology programme. They advise on support for projects in industry, research associations, the department's own laboratories and in other research organisations. Their membership is made up of senior industrialists, academics and government officials.

15 Research establishments. *National Physical Laboratory* (Teddington, Middx, TW11 OLW, tel 01–977 3222, telex 262344). Focal point of the UK national measurement system and provides measurement standards and calibration services for mechanical, electrical, optical, thermal, radiation, acoustic and other quantities. It gives advice on measurement to industry, government and organisations such as BSI concerned with technical specifications. The laboratory also pioneers a number of key industrial technologies, currently materials applications and information technology. NPL runs the British Calibration Service (BCS) and National Testing Laboratory Accreditation Scheme (Natlas), which provide government-backed accreditation for laboratories of proven competence in industry and elsewhere, and the National Corrosion Service (NCS), which offers advice on corrosion prevention and control.

National Engineering Laboratory (East Kilbride, Glasgow G75 0QU tel East Kilbride (03552) 20222 telex 777888). Research, development, design, consultancy and testing facilities are provided for industry and government in mechanical engineering, including fluid power engineering, microprocessor applications, new forming and fabricating processes including fibre reinforced plastics, manufacturing technology including CadCam, robotics and flexible manufacturing systems, heat exchangers and bioreactors, pumps and fans, flow measurement, stress and design analysis, offshore engineering, wind energy and simulation of full-scale loading for structures and components including seismic qualification testing. The laboratory is equipped with modern, often unique, facilities and has extensive expertise in all the above areas.

Warren Spring Laboratory (Gunnels Wood Road, Stevenage, Herts SG1 2BX, tel (0438) 313388, telex 82250). Undertakes applied research and provides research services, advice, consultancy and facilities for industry, government and local authorities on: bulk materials handling technology for powders, pastes and slurries;

microprocessor based control systems and on-line analytical systems; materials separation, mineral and metallurgical processing and chemical separation technology; biotechnology downstream processing; materials recovery from industry, commercial, and domestic wastes; air and oil pollution, measurements and abatement processes for industry.

Laboratory of the Government Chemist (Cornwall House, Stamford Street, London SE1 9NQ, tel 01–928 7900, technical matters ext 477 or 604, establishment inquiries ext 546). Discharges the statutory responsibility of the Government Chemist. Provides a comprehensive service of consultancy advice and studies based on chemistry, with special expertise on analytical chemistry, for the public sector and, where appropriate, the private sector. Supports the aims of the Department of Trade and Industry through cooperative research and development programmes with industry. Provides support and monitors the department's initiative in biotechnology.

16 Chemicals, textiles, paper, timber and miscellaneous industries. Sponsorship of textiles, man-made fibres, clothing, knitting, leather, footwear, tobacco, chemical, rubber, plastics, technical ceramics, fertilisers, toiletries, paint, pesticides, paper and board, timber, and miscellaneous manufacturing industries including pottery, glassware, cutlery, furniture and toys. Also responsible for the textiles and other manufactures requirements board; and the non-metallic materials and chemicals committee of the materials, chemicals and vehicles requirements board. (ASH).

17 Minerals and metals. Sponsorship of the iron and steel industry, BSC strategy, financing and privatisation. Private sector steel scheme. Benefits to redundant steelworkers under ISERB scheme. European Community steel policy. Sponsorship of the foundry sectors and of the non-ferrous metal industries. Research and technology in the metals industries. Responsibility for the materials, chemicals and vehicles requirements board. Industrial non-energy raw materials supply policy including mineral development in the UK, and deep-sea mining provisions of UN Law of the Sea Convention. Administration of the Mineral Exploration and Investment Grants Act 1972. Waste management policies and sponsorship of the reclamation industry (ASH).

18 Shipbuilding policy. Policy relating to British Shipbuilders and assistance for shipbuilding. Administration of assistance for shipbuilding. Sponsorship of the shipbuilding, shiprepairing, mobile offshore installation, boat building, slow-speed diesel engine, marine equipment and hovercraft industries. Support for technological development in marine industries (ASH).

19 Vehicles. Sponsorship and technical matters relating to the motor car, bus, commercial vehicles, electric vehicles, motor and pedal cycle, tractor, agricultural machinery, caravan and trailer industries, together with the associated engine and component industries, garage and repair equipment, and car hire. (ASH).

20 Mechanical and electrical engineering. Encouragement of the application of advanced manufacturing technology (including robots, flexible manufacturing systems and computer-aided design and manufacturing techniques) in UK industry. Sponsorship of the following industries: electrical power generation, transmission and distribution plant; industrial electrical equipment and cables; electric motors and control gear; lighting; mining machinery; wind energy and solar power; batteries; power semi-conductors; process plant; foundry equipment; mechanical handling; construction equipment; fluid power equipment; metal containers; machine tools; manufacturing machinery; domestic electrical appliances; railway equipment; heating, ventilating, air conditioning and refrigeration equipment; bearings; industrial fasteners; drop forgings, and miscellaneous mechanical engineering products. (ASH).

21 General policy. Industrial and commercial implications of domestic economic, fiscal and financial policies. Departmental implications of government policies not specifically covered elsewhere in the department, eg policies on privatisation, energy, pay, pensions, labour and industrial relations, health and safety, environmental protection, physical planning and infrastructure. Departmental planning against civil emergencies. Government initiative on public purchasing policy. Policy and legislation on competition, including monopolies, mergers and restrictive practices. Departmental interest in EC competition rules. (V).

22 Alvey directorate. Established to direct the advanced information technology research and development programme proposed by the Alvey report. The Alvey programme, jointly funded by DTI, Ministry of Defence, the Science and Engineering Research Council and industry, is concentrating on the four key technologies highlighted by the report as being the basis for future information technology systems: intelligent knowledge-based systems, man-machine interfaces, software engineering and very large scale integration. Application of these technologies will be explored in 'demonstrator' projects, and a communications infrastructure for programme support will be established. The directorate is also responsible for liaison with EC Esprit programme. (MT).

23 Financial services and companies. Matters concerning the commercial competitiveness of the financial services sector generally. Regulation of the securities industry; investor protection; accountancy questions. European Community financial services and companies legislation; administration, consolidation and review of the Companies Acts. Statutory investigations and inquiries into companies (S). Companies Registration Offices, Cardiff and Edinburgh, and London search room (CO).

24 Consumer affairs. General responsibility for consumer protection matters, the nationalised industry consumer councils and the National Consumer Council, Government support for the Citizens Advice Bureaux service. Liaison with the Office of Fair Trading on the consumer protection provisions of the Fair Trading Act. Trade Descriptions Acts 1968 and 1972 including origin marking. Sale of Goods Act 1979. Supply of Goods and Services Act 1982 and other consumer legislation. Product liability. Certification trade marks and hallmarking policy. Liaison with trading standards departments of local authorities. International aspects of consumer affairs. Weights and measures trnsactions; regulations and orders; metrication; unit pricing. Sponsorship of the advertising industry and general issues on advertising standards. Consumer credit Estate agency. Safety of consumer goods, including fireworks. (MT).

25 Insurance. Administration of the Insurance Companies Act 1982 including the authorisation and supervision of insurers. Lloyds. Other matters affecting the home and overseas interests of British insurers including work in intergovernmental institutions, eg EC, OECD and Unctad. (S).

26 Insolvency service. All aspects of insolvency administration, including the winding-up of companies under the Companies Acts and the failures of individuals under the Bankruptcy and

Deeds of Arrangement Acts and the Insolvency Act 1976. Administration of the Official Receivers Service in the High Court and provincial offices. Supervision of liquidators and trustees; accounting for and management of funds. Insolvency matters affected by EC legislation and draft bankruptcy convention (BR).

27 British Overseas Trade Board. President, Secretary of State for Trade and Industry. The board's members are drawn mainly from industry and commerce with members also representing the interests of the chamber of commerce movement, the Confederation of British Industry and the Trades Union Congress. It also has officials from the Department of Trade and Industry, the Foreign and Commonwealth Office and the Export Credits Guarantee Department. The board advises the government on matters of overseas trade and directs the government's export promotion services on behalf of the Secretary of State for Trade and Industry. (V).

28 Overseas trade divisions. The Overseas trade divisions are responsible for the promotion and protection of the UK's trading interests overseas. The divisions provide specific services for exports, advice on conditions in overseas markets, deal with bilateral commercial relations with overseas countries and have responsibility for country-related export promotion. They report to a deputy secretary who is also the chief executive of the BOTB. Division 1 (Projects and export policy) deals particularly with major capital projects Divisions 2, 3, and 4 contain individual market branches. With the exception of the Exports to Europe Branch these market branches deal with bilateral inter-governmental commercial relations with the countries for which they are responsible. They have responsibility for country-related export promotion and provide advice on conditions in overseas markets. They guide the work of the commercial staff in UK embassies, consulates, and high commissions abroad Market branches are the focus for briefing for exporters and others on politico-economic conditions, tariffs and regulations, market prospects, and the climate for investment. The branches can provide information on BOTB services in general and deal specifically with requests for the market advisory services, and business visitors. In consultation with the BOTB's area advisory groups and commercial staff overseas the market branches have responsibility for developing programmes of support for UK exporters. The branches handle inquiries from business visitors from their area and are involved in the specifically market-related work of the other export promotion services. Experienced exporters with specific questions about individual markets may wish to approach the market branches direct, while others will find it more convenient to make initial contact with one of the 10 BOTB regional offices. In England these are located in the regional offices of the Department of Trade and Industry (see page 153–4) Division 3 also contains branches responsible for the BOTB's specific export services and Division 2 contains the Export Licensing Branch.

Projects and exports policy division (Overseas trade 1). Responsible, in collaboration with other departments, for integrating the full range of government services in support of industry's pursuit of capital projects overseas. This involves coordinating the use, as necessary, of a number of possible instruments such as ECGD insurance and credit, overseas aid, particularly the aid and trade provision, the overseas projects Fund and several other measures which may in certain circumstances be applied to work associated with export projects. The division may also be instrumental in organising diplomatic backing at official and ministerial level for major contracts. Apart from its main work on individual projects, the division is responsible for a number of policy aspects connected with major projects such as the availability of export financing, competitors practices and selective bidding. The division provides the secretariat for the Overseas Projects Board whose role is to provide a means of closer communication between industry and government on major project business, and to advise on all matters of interest in the projects field and on methods to be adopted in pursuit of specific projects overseas.

World Aid Section provides advance intelligence on projects financed by the international aid agencies (eg the World Bank, the European Development Fund), as well as guidance on their overall activities and future plans (V).

Overseas trade division 2. Market branches responsible for trade promotion and commercial relations with north America, China, Japan, Korea, Taiwan, South-Asian subcontinent, south-east Asia and Australasia. It is supported by eight BOTB area advisory groups made up of businessmen and officials who advise on trade promotion in the various areas. The division also has responsibility for handling problems arising from the exercise by other countries of extra-territorial jurisdiction in commercial matters, policy on Security export controls (V) and the export licencing branch (MT).

Overseas trade division 3. The following branches are within this division:

Administration and Finance Branch is responsible for the development of the BOTB's export services, for the 'Overseas attachment training scheme' and training on BOTB services and for financial control of export promotion activities. It also contains the British Overseas Trade Board Publicity Unit which publicises the board's export services, keeps the British press informed of important trade events overseas and helps exporters obtain publicity for their products and services abroad.

The head of the branch is also secretary of the BOTB (V).

Fairs and Promotions Branch supports groups of British exporters participating at overseas trade fairs through the joint venture and British pavilion schemes, organises all-British fairs and symposia overseas and provides support for overseas store promotions. The branch also provides information on overseas trade fairs, and supports groups of British businessmen visiting certain overseas markets through the outward missions scheme. It provides overseas promotional support for UK trade fairs, liaises with UK exhibition centres and trade fair organisers and arranges inward missions and VIP visits. (DB).

Exports to Europe Branch is the market branch for the promotion of UK exports to western Europe and works closely with the BOTB's European trade committee, one of the BOTB's advising groups. (V).

Export Data Branch is responsible for the Export Intelligence Service (E), a computer-based service providing subscribers with details of specific export opportunities and market intelligence on a selective basis. It is also responsible for the collection, storage and dissemination of information on markets and marketing methods: specific services include the Product Data Store (a central 'bank' of product and industry-based market information which can be consulted by the public), and *Hints to Exporters* booklets. It sponsors the Simplification of International Trade Procedures Board (Sitpro) and operates the Export Marketing Research Scheme and the Market Entry Guarantee Scheme. (V).

East European Branch is responsible for trade promotion and commercial relations with the USSR and Eastern Europe, including Yugoslavia. The branch is supported by the East European trade council and the Anglo-Yugoslav trade council. (V).

Overseas trade division 4. Market branches responsible for trade promotion and commercial relations with middle east, Latin America, the Caribbean and Africa. The Division also supervises the export work of the DTI regional offices. It is supported by six BOTB area advisory groups. (V).

29 European commercial and industrial policy. Community industrial (inc. state aids) and internal market policy questions; rights and obligations under the Treaty of Rome; bilateral relations with western European governments. Enlargement of the community and preferential trade agreements. OECD, industrial science and technology policy questions. (V)

30 International trade policy. Responsible for matters of general external trade policy (mainly now handled through the EC) including Gatt and Unctad, for policies towards international investment and multi-national enterprises, and for industrial aspects of work of Unido. It also deals with anti-dumping cases (guidance, as now mainly handled through the EC commission), protective action against disruptive imports and administration of import licensing, import duties, duty reliefs and suspensions, Generalised Scheme of Preferences (GSP), origin rules, textile trade policy (under the multi-fibre arrangement and associated agreements), and general questions arising out of EC common customs tariff. It coordinates UK policy on multilateral work towards removing barriers to trade in services. (V).

31 Personnel management. Responsible for the personnel management of all the staff of the Department of Trade and Industry, their conditions of service, pay, superannuation, discipline, security, welfare and training; public appointments and honours, and the Queen's Award Office which administers the scheme for the Queen's awards for export and technology. (S).

32 Management services and manpower. Responsible for management services, operational research, complementing and staff inspection, departmental computerisation and information technology applications, industrial relations, contracts for advisory services, libraries, translation services, forms control, accommodation, supplies and office services. (S).

Statistics and Market Intelligence Library (Smil). A reference library for the use of the departments and the public of material on overseas markets, including large collections of economic and general statistics, mail order catalogues, overseas market surveys and development plans, and overseas trade and telephone directories (V).

33 Finance and resource management. Accounting and overall financial policy and control with particular reference to value for money. Secretariat to the Resource Management Group. Coordination of response to the financial management initiative. Coordination and preparation of public expenditure survey forecasts and departmental estimates; and central monitoring of expenditure. Control of manpower numbers and costs. Liaison and coordination for the National Audit Office, Public Accounts Committee and other parliamentary select committees. (K).

34 Solicitor's department. Acts as adviser on legal matters involved in the work of the Department of Trade and Industry, and the Export Credits Guarantee Department. It is responsible for drafting all subordinate legislation, and for prosecutions arising from department-administered acts. (ASH)

35 Economics. Economic division 1 works on private manufacturing industries, technology and regional policy (ASH). Economics division 2 advises on domestic macro-economic issues, trade policy (V), competition policy and nationalised industries (ASH).

36 Statistics. Two divisions provide a statistical service to the department. Statistics division 1 is concerned mainly with manufacturing industry and statistics of company accounts. (MT). Statistics division 2 is concerned with international trade (V), tourism, overseas investment, expenditure on research and development, and statistics relating to the service secotors. (S).

37 Business Statistics Office. (Government Buildings, Cardiff Road, Newport, Gwent, NPT 1XG, tel (0633) 56111 ext 2973). The government's main agency for collecting and processing official business statistics which are published in the form of Business Monitors (see p.168) BSO also provides statistical advice to government departments and other public bodies on movements in the producer price index; capital expenditure and stocks; and retailing and wholesaling.

38 Internal audit branch. Examines all systems of control, financial and otherwise, established by management to secure, as far as practicable, the propriety of transactions, the accuracy and reliability of the department's records and to safeguard assets including debts, equipment, stores and money. Internal audit has regard to the need for management to monitor efficiency, economy and effectiveness in the use of resources in all areas. (EB).

39 Information. Public presentation of departmental policies, activities and services through press, radio and TV. (V). Publicity and promotional campaigns. Publications including *British business, In business now,* Prestel service. (MT).

40 Policy planning unit. Advises ministers and senior officials on objectives and policy, especially on topics which raise questions of priority or cross divisional boundaries. Responsible for coordinating work to define departmental aims and divisional objectives, keeping these under review and advising on the adequacy of the machinery and programmes for achieving them. It normally reports to the permanent secretary. (V).

41 Parliamentary branch. Responsible for coordinating the department's parliamentary work – public and private bills, subordinate legislation (except select committees) and parliamentary questions (V).

42 National Weights and Measures Laboratory Design approval of trade weighing and measuring equipment and the calibration of weights and measures for local authorities, trade, industry and others. Regulations on weighing and measuring equipment and orders on goods under the Weights and Measures Act 1963 and European Communities Act 1972. Representation in the International Organisation for Legal Metrology (OIML) and other international bodies. (CS).

London addresses and telephone numbers

Code	Address
V	1 Victoria Street, SW1H 0ET. Tel 01–215 7877, telex 8811074/5.
VA	20 Victoria Street, SW1H 0NF. Tel 01–215 7877, telex 8811074/5
ASH	Ashdown House, 123 Victoria Street, SW1E 6RB. Tel 01–212 7676, telex 8813148
AT	Atlantic House, Holborn Viaduct, EC1N 2HD. Tel 01–583 8931, telex 22805
BR	2–14 Bunhill Row, EC1Y 8LL. Tel 01–606 4071.
BP	29 Bressenden Place, SW1E 5DT. Tel 01–213 3000, telex 8813148
CHA	Charles House, 375 Kensington High Street, W14 8QH. Tel 01–603 4644, telex 25991
CO	Companies House, 55–71 City Road, EC1Y 1BB. Tel 01–253 9393.
CS	26 Chapter Street, SW1P 4NS. Tel 01–211 3000.
DB	Dean Bradley House, 52 Horseferry Road, SW1P 2AG. Tel 01–212 7676, telex 297121
E	Lime Grove, Eastcote, Ruislip, Middlesex HA4 5SG. Tel 01–866 8771, telex 888013
EB	Ebury Bridge House, 2–18 Ebury Bridge Road, SW1W 8QD. Tel 01–730 9678, telex 297124/5/6
K	Kingsgate House, 66–74 Victoria Street, SW1E 6SJ. Tel 01–212 7676, telex 297124/5/6
MT	Millbank Tower, Millbank, SW1P 4QU. Tel 01–211 3000, telex 8811074/5
P	25 Southampton Buildings, WC2A 1AY. Tel 01–405 8721, telex 266959
S	Santuary Buildings, 16–20 Great Smith Street, SW1P 3DB. Tel 01–215 7877, telex 881107/5
TM	Thomas More Buildings, Royal Courts of Justice, Strand, WC2A 2JY. Tel 01–405 7641.
WBH	Waterloo Bridge House, Waterloo Road, SE1 8UA. Tel 01–275 3000, telex 261969

II Index to Responsibilities in DTI Headquarters

The numbers relate to the Divisional entries in section I.

III Regional Network

A map showing the regional structure used by the DTI is overleaf.

A England

The regional network of the Department of Trade and Industry is based on seven regional offices in England. The regional offices represent the department in its dealings with industry, local authorities, the regional offices of other government departments and other local bodies and organisations. They are responsible for administering sections 7 and 8 of the Industrial Development Act 1982 and are also involved in other aspects of regional industrial development, including the promotion and administration of 'Support for Innovation', a general support facility for promoting research and development. The regional offices handle export promotional work. The regional offices also serve the Department of Energy.

North east: Northumberland, Tyne and Wear, Cleveland and Durham. Regional Office: Stanegate House, 2 Groat Market, Newcastle upon Tyne NE1 1YN, (0632) 324722, telex 53178.

North west: Cheshire, (excluding Widnes, Runcorn, Wirral, Chester), Lancashire, (excluding West Lancashire District), Merseyside, Greater Manchester, St Helens, High Peak District of Derbyshire and Cumbria. Regional Office: Sunley Buildings, Piccadilly Plaza, Manchester M1 4BA, 061–236 2171, telex 667104. Merseyside Sub Office: Graeme House, Derby Square, Liverpool L2 7SU, 051–227 4111 telex 628474.

Yorkshire and Humberside: North, South and West Yorkshire and Humberside Regional Office: Priestley House, Park Row, Leeds LS1 5LF, (0532) 443171, telex 557925.

West Midlands: Shropshire, West Midlands Metropolitan County, Staffordshire, Warwickshire, Hereford and Worcester. Regional Office: Ladywood House, Stephenson Street, Birmingham B2 4DT, 021–632 4111, telex 337919.

East Midlands: Nottinghamshire, Derbyshire (except High Peak District), Leicestershire, Lincolnshire and Northamptonshire. Regional Office: Severns House, 20 Middle Pavement, Nottingham NG1 7DW, (0602) 506181, telex 37143.

South west: Cornwall (including Isles of Scilly), Devon, Somerset,

Regional Offices of the DTI

Wiltshire, Gloucestershire, Avon and Dorset. Regional Office: The Pithay, Bristol BS1 2PB, (0272) 291071, telex 44214.
South West Industrial Development Office: Phoenix House, Notte Street, Plymouth PL1 2HF, (0752) 21891–5, telex 45494.

South east: Greater London, Kent, Surrey, East Sussex, West Sussex, Hampshire, Isle of Wight, Bedfordshire, Berkshire, Buckinghamshire, Essex, Hertfordshire, Oxfordshire, Cambridgeshire, Norfolk and Suffolk. Regional Office: Ebury Bridge House, 2–18 Ebury Bridge Road, London, SW1W 8QD, 01–730 9678, telex 297124/5/6).

B Scotland, Wales and Northern Ireland
The Industrial Development Division of the Industry Department for Scotland (IDS) in Glasgow and the Welsh Office Industry Department (WOID) in Cardiff, in addition to exercising industrial functions which are the responsibility of the Scottish and Welsh Secretaries of State, carry out certain functions for the Department of Trade and Industry on an agency basis. They provide services for British exporters. In Northern Ireland the Department of Economic Development has overall responsibility for industrial matters. The Industrial Development Board for Northern Ireland is a specialised arm of the Department of Economic Development and its responsibilities include the provision of export services.

Scotland: Industrial Development Division of the Industry Department for Scotland, Alhambra House, 45 Waterloo Street, Glasgow G2 6AT, 041–248 2855, telex 777883.

Wales: Department of the Welsh Office, Welsh Office Industry Department, Crown Building, Cathays Park, Cardiff CF1 3NQ, (0222) 825111, telex 498228.
District office for North Wales: Government Buildings, Dinerth Road Colwyn Bay, Clwyd LL28 4UL, (0492) 44261.

Northern Ireland: Industry services, Department of Economic Development, Netherleigh, Massey Avenue, Belfast BT4 2JP, (0232) 63244, telex 747152. *Export services* Industrial Development Board for Northern Ireland, IDB House, 64 Chichester Street, Belfast BT1 4JX, (0232) 233233, telex 747025.

C Small Firms Service
The Department of Trade and Industry administers the small firms service through regional centres which provide small businesses with a free information service covering a wide range of subjects from sources of supply to government legislation. In addition a

counselling facility is available whereby small firms can discuss their plans and problems with an experienced businessman should the inquiry be beyond straightforward sources of information or require detailed or specialist guidance. Counselling is available at a network of 92 area counselling offices. Regional centres may be contacted by dialling 100 and asking the operator for Freefone Enterprise.

Small firms centres

East Midlands: Severns House, 20 Middle Pavement, Nottingham NG1 7DW, (0602) 581205.

South east: Ebury Bridge House, 2–18 Ebury Bridge Road, London SW1W 8QD, 01–730 8451; Carlyle House, Carlyle Road, Cambridge CB4 3DN (0223) 63312; Abbey Hall, Abbey Square, Reading RG1 3BE, (0734) 591733).

South west: 5th Floor, The Pithay, Bristol BS1 2NB, (0272) 294546).

North east: Centro House, 3 Cloth Market, Newcastle upon Tyne NE1 3EE, (0632) 325353).

North west: 3rd Floor, 320–325 Royal Exchange Buildings, St Ann's Square, Manchester M2 7AH, 061–832 5282; Sub-office, Graeme House, Derby Square, Liverpool L2 7UJ, 051–236 5756.

West Midlands: Ladywood House, Stephenson Street, Birmingham B2 4DT, 021–643 3344.

Yorks and Humberside: 1 Park Row, City Square, Leeds LS1 5NR, (0532) 445151).

Scotland and Wales: In Scotland the service is operated by the Scottish Development Agency. In Wales the service is operated in association with the Welsh Office and counselling is provided through the Welsh Development Agency.
Scotland: 120 Bothwell Street, Glasgow G2 7JP, 041–248 6014.
Wales: 16 St David's House, Wood Street, Cardiff CF1 1ER, (0222)396116.

IV Export Credits Guarantee Department

PO Box 272, Aldermanbury House, Aldermanbury, London EC2P 2EL 01–382 7000, telex 883601 and at Crown Building, Cathays Park, Cardiff CF1 3NH (0222) 824100, telex 497305. A separate government department responsible to the Secretary of State for Trade and Industry, ECGD provides credit insurance for UK exporters against non-payment-risks, guarantees to banks for export finance, insurance against political risks on new overseas investments, and support for performance bonds.

Headquarters organisation
Secretary and head of department: J. Gill; Project underwriting: R.T. Kemp; Comprehensive guarantees: D.C. Smith; County policy, overseas investment insurance, international relations: D.H. Twyford; Finance and claims: F.J. Chapman (principle finance officer).

Project underwriting (R.T. Kemp): Specific supplier credit guarantees, buyer credits and lines of credit, guarantees for exports of ships, arms, aircraft, overseas construction work for Australasia, far east, China, Indian subcontinent and Indo-China, middle east and north and west Africa.

Country policy (D.H. Twyford): ECGD's assessment of overseas countries' politico-economic situations.

Overseas investment insurance (D.H. Twyford): Insurance of new overseas investment against political risks.

Project underwriting (D.H. Twyford): specific supplier credit guarantees, buyer credits and lines of credit; guarantees for overseas construction work for north, central and south America, western Europe, Israel, eastern bloc markets, southern Africa and Nigeria (excluding aerospace arms and ships business); insurance against some of the risks of consortium members' insolvency (contracts £20m or more) or withdrawal (contracts £50m or more). Guarantees for specific services (consultancies, knowhow, leasing, etc) for all markets.

International relations: (direct responsibility of the secretary). ECGD's relations with export credit authorities overseas; international credit authorities overseas; international export credit agreements; aid and trade provisions; cost escalation cover (scheme discontinued).

Export financing: (direct responsibility of the secretary). Export financing policy, including foreign currency financing, specific supplier and buyer credit policy. Cover against exchange rate risk between tendering and award of contract.

Comprehensive guarantees (D.C. Smith): Supplier credit insurance for continuous business by manufacturers, merchants, confirming houses or overseas subsidiaries of UK firms, involving exports of raw materials semi-manufactures, consumer goods, consumer durables, production-line equipment and engineering goods. External trade. Overseas stockholding. Finance contracts (overseas banks) endorsement and associated borrower endorsement. Computer services.

Regional organisation
City of London: PO Box 46, Clements House, 14–18 Gresham Street, London EC2V 7JE, 01–726 4050.
Croydon: Sunley House, Bedford Park, Croydon, Surrey CR9 4HL, 01–680 5030.
Belfast: Windsor House, 9–15 Bedford Street, Belfast BT2 7EG, 0232 231743.
Birmingham: Colmore Centre, 115 Colmore Row, Birmingham B3 3SB, 021–233 1771.
Bristol: 1 Redcliffe Street, Bristol BS1 6NP, (0272) 299971.
Cambridge: Three Crowns House, 72–80 Hills Road, Cambridge CB2 1NJ, (0223) 68801.
Glasgow: Fleming House, 134 Renfrew Street, Glasgow G3 6TL, 041–332 8707.
Leeds: West Riding House, 67 Albion Street, Leeds LS1 5AA (0532) 450631.
Manchester: Townbury House, Blackfriars Street, Salford M3 5AL, 061–834 8181.

Finance and claims (F.J. Chapman): Financial policy and accounts, parliamentary estimates, premium reviews, claims; guarantees to banks; guarantees for performance bonds on capital goods contracts worth £250,000 or more.

Secretariat (direct responsibility of the secretary): ECGD's parliamentary work, policy coordination, liaison with Export Guarantees Advisory Council, publicity.

APPENDIX 4

Government Publications and how to trace them

Introduction

Government departments, the structure and senior staff of which are set out in the *Civil Service Yearbook*, produce an extensive range of publications and many are of value and relevance to industry and commerce. They are, however, issued in a variety of ways and this can often make for difficulties in tracing and obtaining them. Her Majesty's Stationery Office (HMSO) is an obvious and well known source for such documents. However they are not all available from "The Stationery Office". In practice government publications if we interpret the word government rather broadly can be divided into three main categories:

I. Those which are published by and sold through HMSO. These are termed "HMSO publications".
II. Those which are published, distributed and sold by government departments. These are sometimes known as "departmental" or "non-HMSO publications".
III. Those which are published and issued by official bodies (eg nationalised industries) and local government.

The publication *Business and Government: A monthly survey of official publications for Business and Industry* cuts across these groups by making an annotated selection from all categories. Available from Alan Armstrong & Associates Ltd in association with HMSO, 72 Park Road, London NW1 4SH. Annual subscription including postage £27.50.

This appendix attempts to guide the reader through the catalogues of the different types of publication and gives advice on how to obtain copies of them. It is particularly concerned with those publications falling into categories I and II above. In cases of difficulty, assistance can often be sought by visiting or telephoning public reference libraries or from the library of the government department concerned. The addresses of the government libraries are given in the Guide to Government Department and other Libraries (see III, F below).

I HMSO Publications

HMSO publishes and prints on behalf of parliament, government departments and other national bodies. It also acts as an agency to sell publications on behalf of other British and international organisations. HMSO issues a number of lists and catalogues as guides to the numerous publications it publishes or sells.

A Lists/Catalogues

Daily List: A daily catalogue of all new HMSO publications, arranged as follows: Parliamentary and HMSO publications, International Organisation publications, for which HMSO acts as UK sales agent, Statutory Instruments and Northern Ireland publications.

Monthly Catalogue: Lists and indexes all HMSO publications issued during the month except statutory instruments and those of International Organisations for which HMSO acts as UK sales agent. This monthly catalogue later forms the Annual Catalogues below.

Annual Catalogue: Lists and indexes all HMSO publications issued in the calendar year including the publications of certain British organisations for which HMSO acts as the UK sales agent.

International Organisations Annual Catalogue: Lists all publications issued in the calendar year by the international organisations for which HMSO has acted as the UK sales agent.

Consolidated Indexes: Five-yearly indexes to each of these annual catalogues. Indexes for 1936 to 1975 are out of print. The index for 1976 to 1980 is still available.

Index to Chairman of Committee: Quarterly. Lists the Chairman of committees the reports of which have been published or sold by HMSO.

Statutory Instruments: A list is published monthly and finally annually. The index in the monthly issues cumulates throughout the year. A list of statutory rules of Northern Ireland has appeared in each issue since April 1983.

List of Non-Parliamentary Publications Sent for Press: Free weekly list of titles sent for printing during the preceding week. Available from PC51B, HMSO, PO Box 276, London SW8 5DT.

Prestel: HMSO's Prestel number is 50040. The database includes the current and recent *Daily Lists*, and newsflashes when appropriate, plus details of recent free catalogues available from HMSO. The daily listing of Statutory Instruments (5004015) is the first published source before the appearance of the *Daily List*. (See also III, H below).

Sectional Lists: These free catalogues list currently available parliamentary and non-parliamentary publications for certain departments or subjects. The series now comprises thirty lists which are brought up to date at regular intervals. They include, Energy, Industry and Trade, Department of the Environment, The Civil Service, and Construction. Copies and further information are obtainable from the Publicity Department, HMSO Books, Freepost, Norwich, NR3 1BR.

Nearly all public libraries should hold some HMSO catalogues. Larger reference libraries should have complete collections of HMSO catalogues and of parliamentary publications. The HMSO leaflet *A Guide to Publications and Services* gives details of the HMSO catalogues and subscription and standing order services. The leaflet also gives details of ordering HMSO publications and lists HMSO bookshops and agents in the UK and overseas. All HMSO catalogues give these details. The *Guide* is available free from the Publicity Department, HMSO Books, Freepost, Norwich NR3 1BR.

B HMSO bookshops and their addresses

London: PO Box 276, London SW8 5DT (postal orders only); 49 High Holborn, London WC1V 6HB (personal callers only).

Edinburgh: 13a Castle Street, Edinburgh EH2 3AR

Belfast: 80 Chichester Street, Belfast, BT1 4JY

Manchester: Brazenose Street, Manchester M60 8AS

Birmingham: 258 Broad Street, Birmingham B1 2HE

Bristol: Southey House, Wine Street, Bristol BS1 2BQ

II Government Departmental Publications' Lists

As mentioned in the introduction many government publications are only available directly from the department concerned, and then often from a variety of Departmental addresses. To help guide the public to the appropriate contact, various government departments issue catalogues of their publications which do not appear in the sectional lists issued by HMSO. These catalogues give details of the documents issued and their availability (ie free or priced) and information on how and where they may be obtained. Details of existing catalogues can be found in *Bibliographic Sources for Non-HMSO Official Publications* (see III, E below).

In addition to these individual catalogues, Chadwyck-Healey Ltd compile a *Catalogue of British Official Publications not Published by HMSO*. This covers over 400 official organisations and the majority of the publications listed are available on microfiche from Chadwyck-Healey (see II, I below). Below are listed examples of a few government departments' publication lists.

A Department of Trade and Industry
Departmental publications not sold through HMSO: This list includes material issued by the Department of Trade and Industry, the Department of Energy, the Monopolies and Mergers Commission and the Office of Fair Trading. It appears on a monthly basis and can be found in the journal *British business* on the second Friday of each month.

Publications . . .: a list of documents not sold by HMSO: 1983, latest edition. Free. This is an annual list of documents issued by the Department of Trade and Industry, the Department of Energy, the Monopolies and Mergers Commission and the Office of Fair Trading. Available from Department of Trade and Industry, Headquarters Library, Room LG30, 1 Victoria Street, London SW1H OET.

B Department of Energy
See also above under A.
Department of Energy publications in print. Free. Issued annually and includes items which are published both departmentally and by HMSO. Available from Department of Energy, Library, Room 1020, Thames House South, Millbank, London SW1P 4QJ.

C Department of the Environment/Department of Transport
Issue a number of publications lists – the principal one being *DoE/DTp annual list of publications* £1.50 or £3.00 with the 'monthly supplements'. Includes publications published both departmentally and by HMSO. Available from DoE Sub-library, Building 6, Victoria Road, South Ruislip, HA4 ON2.

D Health and Safety Executive
There are two main lists:
Publications catalogue. £6.50, available from HMSO. Issued annually and includes publications which are published by HMSO.

Publications in series. Free. A catalogue of HSE publications issued in series. Available from Health and Safety Executive, Safety Engineering Laboratory, Library, Red Hill, Sheffield S3 7HQ.

E *Home Office*
Home Office list of publications. Free. Annual list which does not include those departmental publications issued by HMSO. Available from Home Office, Library, Room 1003, 50 Queen Anne's Gate, London SW1 9AT.

F *Property Services Agency*
PSA in print. 1982 latest edition, new edition in preparation. £3.70, available from HMSO. Includes items which are published both by the department and HMSO.

III General Guides

There are a number of general books published to guide users to the range of publications issued by HMSO, goverment departments and official bodies. Below is a list of the most useful. Annotations are included where necessary.

A *ASLIB Directory*: edited by E.M. Codlin. *Vol. 1*. Information sources in science, technology and commerce. 5th edn. ASLIB, 1982. 789pp. £46. *Vol. 2*. Information sources in the social sciences, medicine and the humanities. 4th edn. ASLIB, 1980. 871pp. £40. Organisations covered include the very large and very small, which provide information services in the above subject fields. Brief details of the organisations listed include the subject coverage of the organisation, special collections or information services and details of any publications issued.

B *British business*: weekly export and industrial news from the Department of Trade and Industry. Annual subscription £70 including postage. HMSO, PO Box 276, London SW8 5DT.

C *British Government Publications*: an index to chairmen and authors; edited by S. Richard. *Vol. 1*. 1800–99. Library Association, 1981. 186pp. £35.
Vol. 2. 1900–40. Library Association, 1975. 174pp. £20.
Vol. 3. 1941–78. Library Association, 1981. 152pp. £27.
Vol. 4. 1979–82. Library Association, 1984. 95pp. £20.

D *British reports, translations and theses received by the British Library Lending Division (including material from the Republic of Ireland)*: Monthly list £45 annually. Available from The British Library Lending Division. Boston Spa, Wetherby, West Yorkshire LS23 7BQ. Lists material which can be difficult to trace such as reports, translations and theses. It lists reports and translations produced by 'government organisations, industry, universities and learned institutions and most doctoral theses accepted at British universities and polytechnics during and after 1970'.

E *Bibliographic Sources for Non-HMSO Official Publications*: 1983. 14pp. Free. Available from The British Library, Reference Division, Official Publications Library, Great Russell Street, London WC1B 3DG.

F *Guide to government department and other libraries*. 1984. 104pp. £10. Available from The British Library, Reference Division, External Relations, Science Reference Library, 25 Southampton Buildings, Chancery Lane, London WC2A 1AW. A selection of special, academic and public libraries are included but the 'guide' mostly concentrates on government departments and agencies. Entries for libraries include details of stock and subject coverage, availability, hours, services and publications.

G *Official publications in Britain*. By D. Butcher. Clive Bingley, 1983. 161pp. £9.50.

H *A guide to government information on Prestel*. July 1984. Free. (Updated at frequent intervals). Available from Central Office of Information, Videotex Services, Room 506, Hercules Road, Westminster Bridge Road, London SE1 7DU.

I *Catalogue of British official publications not published by HMSO*. Chadwyck-Healey Ltd. From 1981 bi-monthly with annual cumulations. £160 annually (1984). Contains publications from over 400 official organisations.
Keyword index to British official publications not published by HMSO. Bi-monthly. (Published on microfiche only). £35 annually (1984) Designed to complement the *Catalogue*. Practically all of the publications listed in both the *Catalogue* and the *Keyword Index* are available on microfiche. They can be ordered as individual publications, price £2.50 per microfiche, by subscription to the complete collection, price £0.60 per microfiche, or by subscription to either of the major collections – science and technology/social sciences, price £0.60 per microfiche, by subscription to the publications of an organisation, price £0.80 per microfiche, or by subscription to one or more subject collections. Chadwyck-Healey Ltd, 20 Newmarket Road, Cambridge CB5 8DT.

J *Councils, Committees and Boards: a handbook of advisory, consultative, executive and similar bodies in British public life*; edited by I.G. Anderson. 5th edn. CBD Research Ltd, 1982. 391pp. £42. (Most public libraries should hold). Entries give brief information on the organisations listed, including terms of reference or duties. Details of regular publications issued or any important 'once-off' publications are also included.

K *Directory of British official publications: A guide to sources*, compiled by S. Richard. Mansell Publishing Ltd, 1981. 360pp. £22.50. (New edition due January 1985).

L *House of Commons weekly information bulletin.* HMSO. Annual subscription £51. Gives information on the work of the House for the week up to the date of issue and forthcoming business for the following week. This includes all public meetings of Select Committees and full details of progress on legislation during the current session.

Select Committee publications and white and green papers are also listed together with European Community draft legislation and other documents which the government has transmitted to Parliament.

M *NEDO in Print.* Summer 1983. 30pp. Free. Lists the reports, films and videos currently available from NEDO. *NEDO in Print Winter 1983/84 supplement.* Free. Available from NEDO Books, Millbank Tower, Millbank, London SW1P 4QX.

N *A guide to British government publications.* by F. Rodgers, H W Wilson Co. 1980. 750pp. $40.

APPENDIX 5

Official Statistics: A Brief Guide

Compiled by Robert Twigger

Introduction

The Government Statistical Service (GSS) produces a vast array of social, economic and administrative statistics. Whilst the GSS is administered centrally from the Central Statistical Office (CSO), the Service has members in each of the main Government Departments who are responsible for the collection and dissemination of data in their fields. Departments' statistical divisions currently contain about 5000 staff of whom about 500 are professional statisticians. As with non-statistical publications (see appendix 4), information is made available to the public in a number of different forms; HMSO publications such as *Social Trends* and *Financial Statistics*, press notices, departmental publications and parliamentary papers and questions. Tracing those statistics which are of interest and obtaining those publications in which the most up-to-date figures appear can be both time consuming and expensive for small and medium-sized firms who do not normally employ specialist staff. This appendix does not attempt to provide a comprehensive guide even to statistics on industry; however, it describes a small number of sources which may be of interest to such companies. A complete guide to official (and some non-official) statistics is provided by the CSO publication *Guide to Official Statistics*. The current (fourth) edition, published by HMSO in 1982 price £25, which runs to over 500 pages, contains a subject-by-subject description of the data that are available, a bibliography and a list of contact points in Government Departments. The fifth edition, which is due to be published in the latter half of 1985, will be similar in format but somewhat briefer.

Before starting a discussion of the data that are available from official sources it is worth noting some that are not. The Statistics of Trade Act 1947, which gives Government Departments the power to collect certain statistics from industry, prohibits the publication of data about individual concerns or data from which information about individual concerns can be derived. For example, the Department of Transport publishes monthly statistics about the total number of motor vehicles registered each month but provides no analysis by manufacturer although these data are readily available from the Society of Motor Manufacturers and Traders. More generally, many trade organisations such as the

SMMT, the Brewers Society and the Wool Industry Bureau of Statistics produce statistical publications which contain data from a combination of trade and official sources.

British business

British business (known as *Trade and Industry* until 1979) is the Department of Trade and Industry's weekly magazine. Each edition contains a statistics section which as well as being a unique source for certain data also summarises information released by the DTI and other departments during the previous week. Although *British business* carries a number of regular series on individual industries; for example, engineering, footwear and textiles, it is probably most useful as a source of more general statistics which provide an overview of the economy. Several of the more important series that appear regularly in *British business* are described below:

Index of Output of the Production Industries
This is the most timely measure of the level of activity in British industry: the monthly article appears in *British business* about seven weeks after the period to which it relates. The *Index* expresses output in each industrial group as a percentage of its level in 1980. Currently the article gives seasonally adjusted figures for about 20 different industrial groups together with broader aggregates, for each year and quarter back to 1980 and each of the last 25 months. In common with all articles in *British business* a contact point at the relevant Goverment Department is given. Other articles, normally published quarterly, contain similar information for Scotland and Wales separately.

The Producer Price Index
This index, formerly known as the *Wholesale Price Index*, measures changes in the prices paid by manufacturing industry for its raw materials and the prices charged for its output. The *Index* is constructed from information about the prices of some 10,000 specific materials and products. Preliminary figures appear in *British business* about six weeks after the end of the month to which they refer and the detailed tables are contained in the following week's issue. This second article includes input and output indices for many of the Standard Industrial Classification (SIC) activity headings within manufacturing and a separate table containing price indices for a wide range of imported raw materials. A further article published each spring contains annual averages for a number of years.

Import Penetration and Export Sales Ratios
Trade figures are normally compiled using a commodity-by-commodity classification; however, in order to produce analyses such as import penetration and export sales ratios, the DTI constructs an approximate industrial breakdown by allocating each commodity to the industry that is mainly responsible for its production. Four ratios are normally calculated:

imports/home demand

imports/home demand plus exports

exports/manufacturer's sales

exports/manufacturer's sales plus imports

Articles in *British business* contain data for the last three years for each of the SIC divisions within manufacturing.

Retail Sales and Credit Business
Both these statistics are indicators of changes in the level of consumer demand. The index of retail sales measures changes in the aggregate value of retail sales and the equivalent changes in the volume of sales after allowance for inflation. Provisional estimates for all retailers appear in *British business* about two weeks after the end of the month to which they refer. A more detailed article which appears some three weeks later contains separate figures for food retailers, mixed retail businesses, clothing, household goods and other nonfood retailers. Statistics on credit business appear in *British business* about five weeks after the end of the period to which they relate. The article gives details of the amount of new credit extended by both retailers and specialist consumer credit grantors such as finance houses, together with the amount of credit outstanding at the end of the month. A separate table gives more details about non-retailer credit; for instance, whether it is fixed-sum or running-account.

Business Monitors

Business Monitors are a group of publications which contain detailed information about individual industries. There are two main series covering the manufacturing, energy, mining and construction industries.

Annual Production Monitors
These monitors contain the results of the Census of Production. This has only been conducted annually since 1970; however, the first census was taken as early as 1907. There is a monitor for each industry identified in the census (usually each 3-digit group of the SIC) and a small number of additional volumes that provide

summary analyses. Although it is called a census, not all production units are surveyed: in 1982 the standard sampling procedure was as follows

Employment in production unit	Production industries	Construction industry
Under 20	not surveyed	not surveyed
20–49	1 in 4	1 in 2
50–99	1 in 2	all surveyed
Over 100	all surveyed	all surveyed
Total forms sent out	18260	5800

The returns for a particular calendar year's Census are based on data for companies' activities during an accounting period ending in the tax year commencing on 6 April of that year. The results are grossed-up so that they refer to the activities of all UK establishments allocated to the industry. Typically the monitors for each industry contain the following information:

1. Number of UK establishments and enterprises allocated to the industry.
2. Total value of sales and other work done (services rendered, capital goods for establishment's own use, goods merchanted or factored).
3. The increase in materials, work in progress and goods on hand for sale during the year and the total value of stocks at the end of the period.
4. The cost of materials purchased and industrial services received.
5. Payments for non-industrial services such as hire of equipment, rent of buildings, insurance, bank charges, vehicle licenses and rates.
6. Acquisitions and disposals of land and existing buildings, plant and machinery and vehicles plus expenditure on new building work.
7. Employment in the industry divided between operatives and administrative, technical and clerical and the aggregate level of wages and salaries paid to each group.
8. An analysis of employment, wages, work done, capital expenditure, stocks and value added by size of establishment.
9. Operating ratios for the industry such as gross and net output per head, ratio of operatives to other staff, ratio of output to stocks and capital expenditure per head.

Quarterly and Monthly Production Monitors

More up-to-date information about individual industries can be obtained from this second group of *Business Monitors*. These provide statistics relating to industries defined by 4-digit activity headings within the SIC. Thus the glass and glassware industry which has a single Census of Production monitor (PA 247) has three associated production monitors; flat glass (PQ 2471), glass containers (PQ 2478) and miscellaneous glass (PQ 2479). Often, as in this case, related production monitors are published in the same volume for convenience. Generally the production monitors are based on quarterly sales enquiries; however, there are four monthly monitors, three cover production in the "car and commercial vehicle"; "wood chipboard and pulp" and "paper and board" industries and the fourth volume contains indices for sales and orders in the engineering industry as a whole. Enquiry forms are sent to all establishments in the industry which have more than a certain number of employees. This cut-off point varies depending on the structure of the industry. Not all the monitors contain the same information but a typical volume may include the following:

1. Sales by those UK manufacturers included in the survey of each of the industry's major products in value and, where feasible, volume terms.
2. The estimated grossed-up sales of all establishments classified to the particular industry including those not included in the survey.
3. Exports and imports of the industry's products in value and, where feasible, volume terms.
4. The HM Customs and Excise tariff/trade codes for each of the industries products.
5. The output producer price index for the industry.
6. An output index for the industry.

Those monitors based on quarterly sales enquiries usually contain figures for the last five quarters and the latest two calendar years.

HMSO Business Data Packages

In 1985 HMSO is to introduce the first of a series of industry related data packages based on floppy discs rather than normal, hard copy publications. The first three industries to be included in this new system will be carpets, electrical appliances and synthetic resins: other industries will be added to the range at a later date. At the time of writing the packages were not publicly available and the following descriptions are based on material released by HMSO. Each package will contain two discs; a data disc and a control disc.

These will be formatted to be compatable with a wide range of micro-computers. The data disc will contain the following information:

1. Total sales for the industry in each of the last ten years broken down by quarter, year and product group.
2. Export and import data for the industry's products over the latest ten year period including quarterly figures by product and annual totals by country of destination/origin.
3. Other statistical data including employment and establishment size for the industry, price index numbers, accounting ratios, import penetration and export sales ratios.
4. A bibliography to HMSO and HSE material relevant to the industry.
5. Names and addresses of those firms classified to the industry.
6. Details of references to the industry in Parliament.

The control disc will contain software which will permit the entry of companies' own information and the manipulation of data; for example, the construction of bar charts and the calculation of growth rates. New data discs will be available each quarter and revised control discs will also be available when the software is up-dated.

Where to obtain publications and what they cost

The following information was correct at January 1985:
British business: price per edition £1.10, annual subscription (UK) £70 from: British business, Freepost, London SW1P 4BR
Business Monitors: the annual subscription for quarterly production monitors is £7.70: each industry monitor for the 1982 Census of Production costs £4. Individual copies of monitors can be obtained from Library Business Statistics Office, Government Buildings, Cardiff Road, Newport, Gwent NPT 1XG. Subscriptions can be arranged via HMSO at HMSO, PO Box 276, London SW8 5DT
Business Data Packages: the annual subscription is to be in the region of £300+VAT per industry, enquiries should be directed to Gordon Robbie, Room 2BO3, HMSO, St Crispins, Duke Street, Norwich NR3 1PD.

INDEX

(*Note*: for detailed index to Department of Trade and Industry see pp 148–152)